Dion Fortune's

GLASTONBURY

By the same author:

Occult study
APPLIED MAGIC and ASPECTS OF OCCULTISM
COSMIC DOCTRINE
ESOTERIC ORDERS AND THEIR WORK and TRAINING
  AND WORK OF THE INITIATE
ESOTERIC PHILOSOPHY OF LOVE AND MARRIAGE
  and PROBLEM OF PURITY
MYSTICAL QABALAH
PSYCHIC SELF-DEFENCE
SANE OCCULTISM and PRACTICAL OCCULTISM
  IN DAILY LIFE
THROUGH THE GATES OF DEATH and
  SPIRITUALISM IN THE LIGHT OF OCCULT
  SCIENCE

Occult fiction
DEMON LOVER
GOAT-FOOT GOD
MOON MAGIC
SEA PRIESTESS
SECRETS OF DR TAVERNER
WINGED BULL

Dion Fortune's
GLASTONBURY

THE AQUARIAN PRESS

First published as *Avalon of the Heart* 1934
This edition, revised and expanded, 1989

British Library Cataloguing in Publication Data

Fortune, Dion
[Glastonbury]. Dion Fortune's Glastonbury:
Avalon of the heart. — Rev. and expanded ed.
1. Somerset. Glastonbury. Antiquities.
Occult aspects
I. Glastonbury II. Title   III. Fortune,
Dion, Avalon of the heart
936.2'383

ISBN 0-85030-793-7

*The Aquarian Press is part of the Thorsons Publishing Group,
Wellingborough, Northamptonshire, NN8 2RQ, England*

Printed in Great Britain by Woolnough Bookbinding Limited,
Irthlingborough, Northamptonshire.

1 3 5 7 9 10 8 6 4 2

Contents

Preface

THE works of the late Dion Fortune were written a long time ago and since then a great deal more has been understood and realized so that many of the ideas then expressed are not now necessarily acceptable. Also, much of what she wrote was written from the viewpoint of the psychic. Psychism is simply one type of inner awareness and there are other types at least as valid and as common. Non-psychic readers, therefore, can translate experience in terms of psychic imagery into terms of their own inner awareness.

The publication of these books continues at present because there is still much of value in them and because they act as valuable pointers to seekers.

Details of the aims and work of the Society of the Inner Light, founded by Dion Fortune, may be obtained by writing (with postage please) to the Secretary at 38 Steele's Road, London NW3 4RG, England.

In December 1942 Dion Fortune wrote:

There are things I wrote of *Spiritualism* twenty years ago which, in the light of wider experience, I would not write today, and to cite these as evidence against me is to deny the possibility of human progress.

'Only I cut on the timber, only I carved on the stone:
After me cometh a builder, tell him I too have known.'

1.

The Road to Avalon

THERE are many different roads leading to our English Jerusalem, 'the holyest erthe in Englande'. We can approach it by the high-road of history, which leads through a rich country, for there is hardly a phase in the spiritual story of the race in which Glastonbury has played no part. Its influence twines like a golden thread through the story of our islands. Wherever mystical forces make themselves felt in our national life, the voice of Glastonbury is heard; never dominating, but always influencing.

Or we can come to Glastonbury by the upland path of legend. In and out twine the ancient folk-stories, full of deep spiritual significance to those whose hearts are tuned to their key. Arthur and his knights come and go. The Graal shines in the night sky above the Tor. The saints live their quaintly beautiful lives amid its meadows. The poetry of the soul writes itself at Glastonbury.

And there is a third way to Glastonbury, one of the secret Green Roads of the soul—the Mystic Way that leads through the Hidden Door into a land known only to the eye of vision. This is Avalon of the Heart to those who love her.

The Mystic Avalon lives her hidden life, invisible save to those who have the key of the gates of vision. The quiet West Country world goes its way. Seed-time and harvest fail not, nor her inexhaustible wells. The pink foam of spring washes over her apple-orchards in its flood; the silver mists of autumn turn her water-meadows once again to a Lake of Wonder. Legend and history and the vision of the heart blend in the building of the Mystical Avalon.

It is to this Avalon of the heart the pilgrims still go. Some in bands, knowing what they seek. Some alone, with the staff of vision in their hands, awaiting what may come to meet them on this holy ground. None go away as they came. Here the veil that hides the Unseen is thin. Here the invisible tides flow strongly; here indeed rests the foot of Jacob's Ladder whereby the souls of men may come and go between the inner and outer planes.

Glastonbury is a gateway to the Unseen. It has been a holy place and pilgrim-way from time immemorial, and to this day it sends its ancient call into the heart of the race it guards, and still we answer to the inner voice.

She is all beauty, our English Jerusalem. The paths that lead to her are ways of loveliness and pilgrimages of the soul. The long road from London spans the breadth of England and leads from one world to another. The narrow and difficult streets of the city give place to the Great West Road—a name magical in its very syllables, and magical too in its great undulating breadth for those who have eyes to see. It turns off from the heavy traffic of Chiswick, lifts to a bridge, and London is left behind. Wide sky stretches over its sunlit, wind-swept spaces, and so broad is it that cloud-shadows skim its surface and it has a horizon of its own. The traffic is swift-moving and silent. We are in another world—a new world, the world that is just dawning over the eastern hills of civilization.

The road leads for a time through the flat valley-bottom of the Thames. Elms are its trees, and the country is unlovely with the marshalled utility of market-gardens, sad because they are falling on decay, for the tide of houses is sweeping over them, and no one cares to tend the worn-out trees when next year's crop may never be gathered.

Soon, however, the country changes; the clay of the valley-bottom gives place to the sand of the Hampshire barrens; birch and fir replace the sordid elms, and we are in a wild and wide land, beautiful as only barren places are beautiful. Heather and gorse climb the rolling slopes and the road runs like a ribbon between them. Here were no ancient rights to make tortuous the public way. No one cared for the sandy barrens, so they were left in their beauty and freedom. The memories of the land are haunted by highwaymen and heavy coaches. The traffic of the south-west went this way. The Great Bath Road lies to the north, and serves another people.

The barrens give way to oaks and rich farming land again, and the first of the Westland signs is seen—a wall, topped with a miniature roof of thatch, or of pantiles blotched with lichen. Hereabouts they build great walls of rammed mud, which stand well so long as the wet can be kept from them; hence the quaint little roofs with their projecting eaves winding along beside the road.

Soon we come to the dividing of the ways. One road keeps its course through the rich lowlands, and the other climbs the heights towards the uplands of England's greatest plain. If we are going to Glastonbury we choose the upland way, and presently the fields give place to the wide, bare turf of the chalk, and dark, sinister bunches of juniper tell us that we are on the Plain.

> Take two twigs of the juniper tree.
> Cross them. Cross them. Cross them.
> Look in the coals of the fire of Azrael!

says the old rune. The dark influences of the juniper overflow the road as the scattered clumps thicken on the slopes. It is indeed the tree of the Dark Angel and the Old Gods.

On this road there still rests the shadow of the Old Gods and their terror. Nature seems so near, and man so much in her power. Primitive man had his townships here; none other has ever dared to meet Nature face to face in this, her place of power. Sheep graze its turf, but no man disturbs its subsoil.

The soul of the place reeks of primitive man, his blood-sacrifices and his dark fears. On every hand lie the barrows of his burying and the tumuli of his sacrifices. Stonehenge stands grey and ominous, dominating the wide grey lands.

The great stones seem to be brooding over their memories, like old men by the fireside whose strength has gone from them and whose minds dwell in the past. The grey stones can never forget—the blood has sunk too deep into them. All round their grim circle the air is heavy and cold with ancient fear. The sun shines grey upon them and the earth feels full of death. They belong to the end of the ancient race, when its light was spent and its vision darkened. Very different is Avebury, the great sun-temple of its glory. Here an invisible sun, formed by the magic of the priests, shines ever into the hearts of men. Here is healing and joy, and a wisdom which is not of this age. Avebury is a temple of the sun, but Stonehenge is a temple of blood, cold and sinister to this day; and those who make the Glastonbury pilgrimage pass swiftly through its heavy shadow, their faces set towards the West.

Lonely sheep-farms, guarded against the gales by beeches, lie remote and rare upon the uplands. From time to time the road passes a low Celtic cross which marks the spot where an aeroplane has fallen and a man been sacrificed to the Race-gods once again.

Then the road dips into beech trees, and the Plain is left behind. Presently the first apple-orchard will appear, and we shall know that we have at last reached the West Country.

The road winds, for it is an ancient way, worn by wandering feet that sought firm ground and good wine rather than the direct route. Above, on the hill-tops, lie the fortresses of primitive man; the earthworks that guarded his wonderful towns, and the terraces called shepherds' steps from which he fought the wolves. The setting sun shines low among the apple-orchards. The smoke of the peat that comes from the Bridgwater marshes smells sweet in the damp of the evening. The houses are all of grey stone, for we are within hauling distance of the Mendips. Great three-horse teams, harnessed in single file, block the way as the timber-wagons go home. Low platforms at the roadside await the clanging milk-lorries that charge down the narrowest lanes of the dairying country. Innumerable cows wander home to their byres, and among the tow-headed children playing at the wayside little black heads begin to appear, for we are approaching the land of an ancient race.

The last barrier of hills is climbed, and the road descends in three great steps towards the alluvial levels that were once all salt-marsh and tidal estuary. The wide flat plain stretches out in the evening light. Smoke hangs over the clustering hamlets that lie thick in this rich land. Here and there on its expanse rise sudden hills, still called islands hereabouts, where some eddy of the slow Severn tide laid down its silt. Upon one side the line of the Poldens guards the levels; upon the other, the Mendips. Beyond is the sea, hidden by the grey mist of distance. In the middle of the plain rises a pyramidal hill crowned by a tower—the Tor of Glastonbury!

There is such magic in the first glimpse of that strange hill that none who have the eye of vision can look upon it unmoved. Each road around Glastonbury has its trysting-place where the Tor first comes into view. Whether from the train it be seen hung high in heaven, its foot among the orchards and red roofs; or whether, seen from the road, it lies far below, in the wide plain lined with willows and water-cuts, never does the magic of the first glimpse fail. What powers the ages have centred upon that strange hill who can say? The ancient Druids knew it; the earliest Christians knew it; and the tradition tells us that 'Avalon has never lacked a seer'.

The foot-hills, full of water-springs, nestle round the

base of the strange pyramidal hill with its grey tower. They are of another order of creation. But one among them has any kinship with the Hill of Vision. One bowl-shaped hill of richest green lies upon its flank. Chalice Hill it is called, and it is reputed to have been the home of the Fisher King, who ever suffered from a grievous wound; and in its heart was the treasury where he kept the Graal.

The grey Tor rises to heaven and the green hill dreams beside it. Between them springs the running red water of the Holy Well; at their feet lies the town with its red roofs and blue peat-smoke. Around stretch the moors with their willows and water-cuts, and the banked straight streams and sluices that can only flow out into the sea at low water. It is a green land, a kindly land, and the Hill of Vision broods above it.

2.

The Avalon of Merlin

TWO legends are wound about Avalon, the legend of the Cup and the legend of the Sword—the cup from which Our Lord drank at the Last Supper, and in which the drops of His Blood were caught; and Arthur's sword, Excalibur, engraved with ancient pagan runes.

Two traditions meet in Avalon—the ancient faith of the Britons, and the creed of Christ. The older, its relics obliterated, its legends bent to a Christian purpose, is shadowy and veiled. Only here and there do we see clearly the lineaments of the ancient creed; but a veiled figure can be seen in the darkness of racial memory, and its dim but awful presence is alive.

There is an Avalon of the Sword which is far older than Avalon of the Cup. Long before the slow-flowing Severn had laid down the silt that gave us the low-lying lands of Somerset, the island of Avalon was an island indeed. In the shallow waters of the brackish lake that surrounded it were the dwellings of an ancient people who found safety from beasts and their fellow-men, no less savage, among the reeds of the great fen of the west. Other tribes of primitive men had their homes in pit-dwellings on the chalky hills of the Pol-dens or in the many caves of the limestone range of the Mendips. All these, from hill-top or marsh, must have seen that strange pyramidal hill of Avalon as we see it to-day. How must it have appeared to primitive man if it so grips the imagination of modern man?

At the foot of the Tor is the wonderful Blood Spring, the iron-laden waters that rise from the oldest rocks, and whose flow never alters, summer or winter, flood or drought. About this well-head is built a chamber of great blocks of stone such as were used at Stonehenge. There is no stone like this in the neighbourhood. A single block of stone forms three sides of the well-mouth, a block so vast that only powerful tackle could handle it, and the masonry fits with the closest accuracy, true-square, perfectly perpendicular. The round well-shaft leads down some fifteen feet to a bed of blue lias gravel, through which rises with powerful flow an unfailing spring.

In the water float misty masses of the colour of stale blood. This is a rare water-fungus, stained by the iron-laden water.

Opening out of the well-shaft is a large chamber of finely hewn stone, square and correctly orientated. As the sun rounds the shoulder of the Tor on Midsummer day a shaft of light shines straight into the inner chamber. In one wall of that chamber is a recess in which a man could just stand. There is a sluice which enables the water to be run off so that the inner chamber can be entered; when the sluice is closed it rapidly refills with the clearest and coldest water, for the flow of the spring is tremendous.

This was never a Christian well, made by holy men for their simple needs. What is this man-sized niche in a well-chamber which can be emptied and filled at will? What is the strange and sinister power which still broods over the Well? This was no fountain hallowed by miracle and vision, but an ancient Druid place of sacrifice, and the upright, man-shaped niche under water shows the nature of the sacrifice. The Fisher King, if he were indeed an historic personage, may have availed himself of the superstitious awe in which such a well would be held, and hidden there the Cup when danger threatened; but this strange well, with its blood-stained waters flowing through reddened channels, is holy to the Old Gods and their dark powers.

The monks, finding it already hallowed by popular veneration, being wise in human nature, adapted it to Christian purposes, as was their wont, and wove about it the story of the Cup; but no one who has eyes to see in the world of men, and the still greater gift of the eye that sees in the inner world, can doubt that at the Well and the Tor we meet the Old Gods face to face.

The Abbey is holy ground, consecrated by the dust of saints; but up here, at the foot of the Tor, the Old Gods have their part. So we have two Avalons, 'the holyest erthe in Englande', down among the water-meadows; and upon the green heights the fiery pagan forces that make the heart leap and burn. And some love one, and some the other.

There can be but little doubt that the priests of the ancient sun-worship had here their holy place. The Tor is a strange hill, and it is hard to believe that its form is wholly the work of Nature. Round it winds a spiral way in three great coils, which was beyond all question a processional way. When did the Christians worship upon high places? Never. But such mounts as this were always sacred to the sun. It is the natural place for a sun-temple, and for the great fires of the kindred fire-worship. The perfectly symmetrical green round of Chalice Hill also looks too perfect to be the work of Nature, and on the opposite flank of the Tor are terraces whose use is not known. They could hardly have been for vine-growing, as they do not face south.

Man's hand has been here, on Tor and Hill and Well, and the hand of men who worked with knowledge and power. The Abbey and Beckary are one world, and the Tor and its Well another, an older, more vital world; and though the Well is dark with blood, the Tor is bright with fire. The Abbey is sanctified by Patrick and Bride and Dunstan, but the Well is sacred to Merlin.

In the days before the Fisher King was made custodian of the Graal, dark Morgan le Fay, half-sister to Arthur and pupil of Merlin, had her dwelling upon Chalice Hill. May not the still surface of the Well, with its great gouts of blood-stained fungus, have been her magic mirror? What could not the witch have seen in that still surface reflecting the stars, with the dead man bound in his narrow niche in the deep well-chamber lending the power of sacrificed life? Her spirit it is that broods over the Well and wakes the eyes of vision in the souls of those who gaze into it.

The history of Arthur passes from heathendom to Christendom and back again. His birth was presided over by Merlin on the wild Cornish cliffs. Some say he was cast at the feet of the mage by a gigantic wave;

others that he was born of the lawless passion of Uther, King of Britain, for Ygrain, wife of Gorlois, King of Cornwall, who for lust of her slew her husband in battle and besieged her castle, taking her by force. Others, again, say that Merlin brought Uther secretly to the queen by a rock-hewn stair in the cliff, in order that the Gates of Life might be opened to the soul of Arthur, who should be the saviour of his people.

All tales agree that Merlin received the new-born child into his hands and took him away to be trained in hiding and secrecy under his own care. Whatever else Merlin may have been, he was not a Christian. He was the High Priest of the Old Gods, the Arch Adept of our race. So, like Moses and Jesus, Arthur made the 'descent into Egypt' and learnt the ancient wisdom of the initiates.

It was to Avalon he came to visit his dark sister, Morgan le Fay, half-human and half-fairy. It was here dwelt the Lady of the Lake and her sister queens, and they guarded the magical Sword as later the three pure maidens guarded the sacred Cup for the Fisher King. This Sword, plunged in a block of stone, awaited the coming of a champion who should draw it forth. Many knights tried their strength and failed, and the land was laid waste by savage beasts and more savage men. Then came Arthur, and the Sword leapt forth in his hand.

One one side of the blade was graven in ancient runes, 'Take me', and on the other, in the language of the day, 'Caste me away'. So it must ever be with the illuminated soul. He must take into his hand the sword of the ancient faith and wield it as true knight till the land is cleansed of its evil, and then he must cast it away in order to take up the sword of the spirit. Only thus shall he heal him of his grievous wounds won in battle, and rest in the green Isle of Avalon,

> Where falls not hail or rain or any snow,
> Nor ever wind blows loudly.

For Arthur of the Sword is not the Arthur of the Table Round, a very peerless Christian knight. By Merlin's hands he was received at birth, and into Merlin's hands he goes when the shadow of death comes upon him. The three queens in their dark barge come through the swaying reeds of the great marsh of Severn after the last battle in Lyonesse; Excalibur is flung into the mere at the bidding of the king; the ancient gods take back their sword again, and the three queens bear Arthur away from the sight of men for ever.

3

The Avalon of the Graal

THERE are two names given the isle among the marshes—Glastonbury and Avalon. The scholars derived the word Glastonbury from its ancient Keltic name of Ynisvitrin, the Glassy Isle, or Shining Isle, and Avalon is believed to mean the Isle of Apples. To those who love her, Glastonbury is her outer name, the name of the little town which is a miniature of English history, whose influence weaves through the weft of its story like a thread in tapestry, giving saint and statesman and scholar to our race.

Ynisvitrin saw the men of the lake villages, marvellously built upon piles among the marshes; she saw the men of the caves under Mendip who came to raid and trade with them. She saw the Romans come and go. She saw the tide of the Norsemen sweep across southern England as far as her encircling hills, there to be turned back, for the sound of fighting has never been heard in the streets of Glastonbury.

Here rose one of the earliest, as one of the greatest, monastic houses in these islands, and here was the light of scholarship and culture kept burning through the Dark Ages when Europe returned again to savagery.

But there is another name to our island, and another story belonging to her—the parable of her spiritual significance. History may tell us that Christianity came to these islands from Ireland, but legend, which enshrines the spiritual heart of history, declares that the Light of the West came to us straight from the place of its rising, and that we were indebted to no intermediaries for its transmission.

After the Last Supper, so the ancient story runs, the owner of the house wherein was the Upper Chamber preserved as a memento the cup that had passed from hand to hand at that sad feast. This cup came into the hands of Joseph of Arimathaea, and in it he caught the drops of blood that fell from Our Lord's wounded side when he came to fetch the Body for burying.

Later, when the Christian Church began to send forth missionaries to the peoples, an angel came to Joseph in a dream, and commanded him to gather about himself twelve disciples and to sail westward till he saw a hill like Mount Tabor, and to land beneath the shadow of that hill and found a Church.

He obeyed, and with the sacred Dish thrust into the girdle of his robe, as was the custom with travelling Syrians, he and his comrades set sail from the seaport of Joppa and steered towards the setting sun. They bore west day by day until they reached the Gates of Gades, and then the wide Atlantic that led to the world's end opened before them, and they perforce turned north, along the coast of Spain, for all navigation was coastwise in those days.

Coming to the Narrow Seas, they struck north across the Channel, and made the landfall of Britain. Then, in obedience to their instructions, they turned as much west as might be, and came cruising up the coast of

Cornwall, with its terrible cliffs, working their way into the Severn estuary.

To this day the Tor is a sea-mark to pilots coming up the Severn. Far over the flat lands it can be seen, and they lay their course by it. Joseph and his comrades saw it as they came up among the silt and sand-banks of the estuary, and recognized its likeness to Mount Tabor. They turned the prow of their boat from its sea-wanderings, and came up the stream among the water-meadows that winds about the base of Wirral, or Weary-all hill, the outlying buttress of Avalon; and here, all weary from their wanderings, the pilgrims landed, and St. Joseph, driving his staff into the ground, declared that here would he found his Church. And the staff, a stout blackthorn, burst into leaf and blossom, although the season was mid-winter, as a sign that Heaven ratified his choice.

On the slope of the long green hill there is a stone commemorating the spot where an ancient thorn-tree had stood, a thorn like none other in the neighbourhood, that never failed to produce blossoms in mid-winter besides its normal flowering in the spring. This marvellous tree was cut down by a Roundhead zealot in Cromwell's day, but slips from the ancient sire had been planted by the monks in the Abbey garden, and also in the graveyard of the parish church, and there to this day they live on, still yielding their blossoms at Christmas for the decoration of the high altar of St. John's. It is, say the botanists, a thorn of a kind only known in the Levant. Away from Glastonbury it soon loses its habit of flowering at Christmas.

The prince of the tribes of that region made these holy

men welcome. There were no massacres here. He gave
them twelve hides of land for their holding, and the little
wattle church they built thereon arose where the great
Abbey now stands. They built themselves a circular
church of withies, and around it they built twelve wattle
cells, one for each hermit, and there they lived in prayer
and meditation, keeping a perpetual watch in the church,
their feet wearing pathways from each cell to the centre,
like the radiating rays of the sun.

Here the Cup of the Last Supper stood upon the altar,
an object of perpetual adoration. Here St. Joseph laid
his bones. Thus was the 'holyest erthe in Englande'
consecrated.

But the times were evil, for the dusk of the Dark
Ages drew on, and men were too wicked to be entrusted
with the sacred relic, so the Fisher King took it to keep
in his treasury, an underground chamber in the heart
of Chalice Hill, that round-topped hill of perfect green
that rises from the flank of the Tor. There the Cup was
guarded by three pure maidens, who watched it day and
night, and only brought forth for high festival, when
it passed from hand to hand in memory of Our Lord,
and His Death upon the Tree. Whosoever drank of it
never thirsted again, for it was to him a well-spring of
the Waters of Life within his soul.

So Glastonbury sank into the darkness of the Middle
Ages; but Avalon lived on in the hearts of men, and the
Arthurian legends wove about her ancient history. Here
came the knights who sought the Graal. They crossed
the little river Brue by Pons Perilis, and watched all
night in the little chapel at the foot of Wearyall Hill,

overlooking the water, where dark temptations came to try the soul. But if he failed not in his watch through the darkness, from here it was that the knight went forth at morn on the last stage of his journey, to be welcomed and rested in the sunny chambers of the Fisher King on his green hill, and to drink from the veritable Cup of Our Lord at the love-feast made in his honour that night. Of those who drank of this Cup not all lived to tell of it. Their souls, fallen into a swoon, were wrapt away to the heights and came not back again.

But the times became more evil, and the twilight darkened to night, and the Fisher King, for greater safety, concealed the sacred Cup in the spring which rose at the foot of the cleft between the two hills. This was no ordinary spring; its waters rise from an immense depth, and in the greatest drought they never alter their flow. They rise through a well-head of cyclopean stones of ancient workmanship, like those of Stonehenge. This was a sacred well of the Druids or ever Christian thought wove legends about it. The waters, charged with iron, run red as blood. But there is no iron nearer than the Mendips. They are icily cold, unaffected by summer or winter. They must come from a great depth and from far away. The name of that spring to this day is the Blood Well.

4.

The Isle of Avalon

IT is not so long since Avalon was an island. An old woman, sitting at the door of her cottage, told me that her grandmother could remember the water coming up the St. Benignus Church when the great dykes burst on Bridgwater Bay, twenty-miles away. All the land about Avalon lies low, some four feet below high-tide mark, and was a salt-marsh until the dykes were built on the bay. The Brue, an unpleasing and sluggish stream, flowing between high embankments, can only empty into the Bristol Channel at half-tide through great swing-sluices that keep back the sea. Everywhere are the water-cuts, draining the meadows, each with its line of pollarded willows. In this part of the world they are called rhines, a name that came over with the Low Country engineers who, bred on a sand-bank, knew the arts of dike and ditch, and won much of England from the sea for our forefathers.

There is a story that the Duke of Monmouth was told by an astrologer to beware of the Rhine, for there he would meet his fate. On the night before the battle of Bridgwater the old prophecy was recalled jestingly, and he declared that he was safe for the moment, at any rate. But it was one of these water-cuts that threw his army into confusion and led to his overthrow.

The water-meadows are of that emerald green only to

be seen where the subsoil water is near to the surface. Travelling through parched lands at midsummer, one knows that Avalon is near by the greenness of the earth. Everywhere are flowers of tree, bush, and herb. The flowers alone are a guide to the wayfarer. Tell me what you have plucked, and I will tell you where you are and which way lies Avalon. Teazles and kingcups and great bulrushes with tails like angry cats belong to the water-meadows. Traveller's joy hangs like smoke over the chalky escarpment of the Polden Hills, and the Mendips have pine and heather on their crests. The hills of Devon, grey on the horizon, have earth as red as blood, and ferns, ferns, ferns! And always and everywhere there are the thorn-trees, white with bloom or red with berries. Indeed, a goodly land, and kindly.

But there is a place that looks like hell by moonlight, and that is where they cut the peats out in the marshes 'over to Ashcott', as we say about here. The soil is jet-black, and the bright green of the lush foliage looks evil and sinister. The road runs high between great water-cuts, and on either side marches the army of the dead—narrow black pyramids of peats, piled high for drying. Much can be forgiven to peat, however, for it smells so sweet in the burning. At evening pale blue spires of smoke ascend from the cottage chimneys and the air is full of incense. Peat is a keeper of the records. It preserves whatever is entrusted to its care. Out among the lowlands, where a slow stream creeps to the sea, low green mounds dotted the fields. Cattle grazed over them and none heeded them. They had always been there. No one thought to ask how it was that these low mounds should mark the green meadows that had once been a mere. One day the plough laid them open, and there was revealed the hard-baked earth of the hearths of ancient man. This was cut through and another hearth was found. And so they lay, hearth below hearth, as ancient man had repaired his dwelling or the waters of the mere had changed their level.

In the ancient days, when the channels kept open by the slow-moving streams were the only ways through the marsh, men built their villages on great oaken piles rammed into the soft ooze. The peat guarded these from decay, and the waters guarded the tribe from its enemies and furnished food.

In ancient days man could only live where he found natural means of defence. In the forests beasts could come upon him unawares, and in the open lands his fellow-men. So he built his wonderful towns with their great stone altars on the bare downs where none could approach unobserved, or else among the marshes where only those who knew the channels from the backwaters could bring the crazy coracles through the maze of reedy creeks.

Civilization began early in the warm and kindly land of the West, and everywhere we find traces of primitive man, his altars and his hearths.

But other than primitive man sought the shelter of the marshes:

> When Rome was sunk in a waste of slaves,
> And the sun drowned in the sea.

The monks alone guarded the ancient books in the day when all fighting men had to turn barbarian in order to meet the barbarian. Like the men who gathered the first grain into earthern storage-pots, they too had to seek shelter from a predatory world. They too made their way along the ancient water-ways to the marshes that gave shelter from enemies.

But the monks loved good gardens and fresh water; they were not content with the brackish pools that had served the lake-dwellers. They knew the ague that shook the men of the marshes. And so they chose to make their home in the apple-isle of Avalon, the group of softly rounded hills that cluster about the base of the Tor that rises like a flame from their midst.

There dwelt the monks in a fair ground, full of good water-springs, and their civilizing and humanizing influence stretched all over the marshes to the far hills where they cut their stone. There they wrote and drew their wonderful books:

> Wrought in the monk's slow manner,
>   From silver and sanguine shell,
> Where the scenes are little and terrible,
>   Keyholes of heaven and hell.

Here lived what little civilization there was in those dark times. Here were the gardens tended, the sick nursed, and the children taught. Still the great grey wall marks the limit of the monks' demesne; still the ancient tithe-barn holds the harvest, the four Evangelists looking to the four quarters of heaven from its roof and keeping an eye on the tithes.

Glastonbury is not only deep-rooted in the past, but the past lives on at Glastonbury. All about us it stirs and breathes, quiet, but living and watching. We can hear its heart beat here if we lay our ear to the earth. Its life-blood moves in the clear springs of Avalon and the slow streams of the marshes. Layer below layer lies the spirit of the past at Avalon, just as the hearths of an ancient people lie among the pools of Meare. We who love can listen, and Avalon speaks.

5.

Avalon of the Keltic Saints

THERE is another atmosphere within the Abbey precincts, as well as that of the medieval Church, which permeates the town like incense. To come from the great nave into St. Joseph's Chapel is to pass from one world to another. Tradition tells us that this beautiful and intricate chapel was built around the ancient wattle church of the earliest Christian missionaries to our islands, and there is little reason to doubt the truth of the tradition.

There was a Christianity in these islands before Rome laid her organizing hand upon them. There was an ancient Keltic Church that knew not the Pope, save as one among many bishops. There were three holy centres in Britain whence the Light of the West was spread, and the greatest of these was Glastonbury.

History tells us that Christianity was first brought to these islands from Ireland, the Isle of Saints, but legend tells us that it came hither directly from Palestine. Be that as it may, it was in Avalon that Christianity first saw the light of day in these islands, and the ancient wattle church was its cradle.

So many holy men have prayed and died at Glastonbury that the spiritual atmosphere is alive and aglow. Their dust, mingling with the earth, sanctifies the very ground beneath our feet. There were no martyrs here till

Henry VIII chose his victims; men sanctified Glastonbury by their living, not their dying.

St. Patrick crossed the Irish Sea in his frail craft
and came here, organizing the solitary hermits under a
discipline. St. Bride, too, sweetest of solitaries, had her
cell at Beckary, a low rise of ground beyond Wearyall.
There she left her weaving-tools behind her, and a few
years ago a bronze bell of most ancient workmanship was
found there by a shepherd, and was given by him to
Chalice Well for the chapel, where its two sweet notes
used to give the call to prayers, morning and evening.
That it was a woman's bell is certain, for the finger-holes
by which it is held are so small that only a woman's
fingers could use them.

St. David came here from Wales, so the story goes,
together with seven other bishops, in order that he might
dedicate the new-built church to the Virgin Mary; but
Our Lady appeared to him in a dream and told him that
her church was already dedicated to her by the sanctity
of the ground, so the good saint blessed the holy men of
the island and departed, giving glory to God.

It was at Beckary that King Arthur, summoned by a
dream while sleeping at the nunnery on Wearyall, saw
the marvellous sacrament wherein the Holy Child was
Himself the sacrifice upon the altar, laid there by His
Mother. It was there, in Bridget's Isle, called 'Little
Ireland', that Our Lady gave to Arthur the wonderful
crystal cross which by him was afterwards given to
Glastonbury Abbey. This crystal cross he graved upon
his shield, silver on green, in memory of the graciousness
of the Queen of Heaven, and later the monks of the

Abbey made it their badge also, and it can be seen to this day quartered with their arms.

There was no real monastic rule in those days. Holy men lived as hermits in holy places, each a law unto himself. Gradually, out of propinquity, some sort of rule crept in. Women were seldom solitaries owing to the dangers of the times, but had perforce to dwell behind strong walls for their own protection. The holy women seem to have had for their own the outlying high ground of Wearyall, with its attendant island of Beckary, for before the great dykes were made along Bridgwater Bay the tide came up to the foot of Wearyall, and all the present moors were a salt-marsh filled with the crying of sea-birds.

There was no regular monastic life at Glastonbury till the Benedictines brought thither their learning and rule. The earliest Christianity in these islands was not Roman, but Keltic, and to the Keltic Christians the Pope was but one bishop among many. Devout men and women carried the light of faith to the wild tribes of the north and the west, but they looked to holy Ireland, not to Rome, for their inspiration. But gradually the influence of Rome asserted itself over all the scattered Churches, and the primitive local customs and traditions were absorbed and unified, till there was one Church in Christendom.

The contemplatives gathered around the Holy Well at Glastonbury were organized under the rule of St. Benedict, and the Abbey walls began to rise, St. Joseph's Chapel actually being built so as to enclose the humble wattle church of the first hermits.

Art and learning came to Glastonbury, and the great

estate that supported them began to be built up, and far out over the moors we find the Abbey arms above the doors of the beautiful old grey stone granges, standing solidly to this day.

Far from London and the turbulent strongholds of barons, protected by its marshes, Glastonbury grew into a garden of Christian life. There was no other spot in these isles that could rival it in length of tradition, for in its first saint it had a link with Our Lord Himself. Century by century the spiritual life of the place grew like a great vine, and that life appears, from all records, to have been of a singular purity.

Glastonbury is sanctified by the prayers and dust of holy men and women. Generation after generation of Englishmen trod the pilgrims' path through the marshes, and the eyes of all Europe turned here as to a holy sanctuary. It is this vivid spiritual life which built the unseen Avalon; it is the warmth of this hearth of faith which warms our hearts to-day when we stand on the 'holyest erthe in Englande'. Her stones are so full of memories that we cannot but remember, and the soul is stirred and thinks of God.

For God has been thought about so much in this island in the marshes, He has been so loved and served, that He is very near, and the veil that hides the sanctuary is very thin. Whether or no God drew near to Glastonbury who shall say? But Glastonbury drew very near to God, and the fragrance of that Presence still lingers.

6.

Wearyall

FROM the outskirts of Glastonbury a long finger of high ground stretches out into the marshes. Upon its northern flank is a little plantation famous for adders; upon its outlying head stands a single oak; for the rest, it is clothed in close-growing, sweet hill-grass, green as only Westland grass is green. Along its southern face winds a narrow road, dipping, rising, bending to the contours of the ground with the perverse disregard of human convenience which is so characteristic of ancient tracks, made before man had got the upper hand of Nature in these isles.

To the north, along the level, runs the modern road to Street, the Quaker factory village among the green water-meadows. The two roads meet at the head of Wearyall hill, where lies the ancient river-crossing, the Pons Perilis of Arthurian legend.

Between them, these two roads tell the story of English history, a story written in the road-maps of our land if we cared to read it. Why does the ancient road wind about the high ground and the modern road go by the fields? Why do they meet at the bridge, and go thence, both together, modern metalling borne on ancient piles, straight as a die to the far Polden Hills, there to climb on to the high ground again and follow its dips and windings to Bridgwater?

In the old days the green meadows around Glastonbury were marshes. To this day they depend upon the dykes on Bridgwater Bay to protect them from the high spring-tides. Between each field are deep water-cuts that discharge into the banked-up rivers. Through these marshy and treacherous places a road could only be carried on an embankment; therefore, as far as might be, the ancient trackways followed the firm ground, the struggle up the steep gradient being less exacting than the struggle through miry bottoms. To-day the marshes are drained by their water-cuts, the ditches are tended like a garden, and the rank salt-marshes where the lake-men had their dwellings are richest pasture-land.

The modern road goes straight through the level fields, but the winding hill-track guards its memories. Beside the modern road the red-brick villas, the petrol pumps, and the tea-rooms spring up. Beside the winding hill-road stand the ancient cottages, built of heavy Mendip stone in vast blocks, some of them colour-washed Reckitt's blue, ochre, and pink. Their low doors open straight on to the pathway of immense flags, six times the size of a London paving-stone. These cottages are very old. There is no trace of Abbey stone in their structure; they stood there and housed their people while the Abbey was the centre of Glastonbury life and men thought it would stand for ever.

In a double row they line the old road as it climbs laboriously on to the hill. Men sought the high ground in the old days to escape the agues of the marshes and the fevers of the narrow alleys and courts of the medieval town. Presently the cottages become a single row, and then cease, and the road goes on alone, dipping and rising over the spurs of the hill, till it drops down sharply to the bridge-head. Ancient and modern ways meet here, for it is the only firm ground for miles. Elsewhere a bridge would have to be met by long abutments, and just as the first gravel ridge on the Thames estuary decided the situation of London, so the detritus of Wearyall decides where modern motor and ancient pack-horse shall cross the Brue. Every road tells its story, would we but trouble to read it; it is never built at random—there is always a human need behind it—and in the abandoned tracks and modern arterial roads we can read the history of industrial England.

The river and the road make of the head of Wearyall a place rich in story. Boats coming up the river find there the first practicable landing-place, and so Joseph of Arimathaea strikes his staff in the earth of Wearyall. The road, borne on piles through the marshes, is a desolate and houseless track until it climbs on to firm land at the head of the long, low hill. Here, therefore, must stand the first hospice for travellers after the weary miles over the bleak marsh road. Here, therefore, it is that the knights of Arthur, on the quest of the Graal, spend the last night of their pilgrimage, for medieval towns close their gates at dusk, and travellers have to lodge without the wall if they arrive after dark. Can we not imagine how the pilgrims, weary from that last long stage across the marshes, must have watched the lights of the Holy City of England gleaming among her hills as they waited for the opening of the barriers at sunrise?

It is said that upon Wearyall the holy women, drawn

to Glastonbury by its sanctity, made their home, away
from the noisome and brawling discord of the narrow
streets of the town. They it was, therefore, who served
the hospice that ministered to the needs of the travellers.
Out beyond the head of Wearyall, on a low islet among
the marshes, was a hermitage of those who desired complete solitude. The marshes protected them from the
intrusion of strangers; the men of the country revered
them; there, under the protection of their own purity,
St. Bride and her gentle companions served and loved God
in the silence of the still brown peat-waters of the meres.

There was a chapel beside Pons Perilis from which the
bridge took its name. It was not the dangers of the river-
crossing that made this spot feared, but the spiritual
terrors that here beset the pilgrim at the final stage of his
journey. Here was the last spot upon which the Devil
could assail him, for beyond lay holy ground, and here
he had perforce to wait through the hours of darkness
when the Devil was abroad. The Knights of the Graal
did not sleep here after their journey across the marshes;
they watched all night before the altar till the old priest
should come to perform the midnight mass—the mass
which appeared to turn into a devilish orgy before their
eyes. It is the old story of the tests of the pilgrim soul,
the last test being the apparent transformation of holy
things into arch-evil.

But if the knights endured without flinching and kept
the long vigil without falling on sleep, in the early morning
there was performed a mass wherein the Son of God indeed
was made manifest to their eyes. Then they passed on
to the holy earth of Avalon, to be feasted by the Fisher

King and shown the Graal with its guard of virgins. And some died of bliss at the sight, and none ever walked with men as man again. The road over Wearyall is the last stage of the Graal pilgrimage.

It was here, at the head of Wearyall, that King Arthur received the crystal cross at the hands of Our Lady—the cross he emblazoned on his shield and banner and under which he fought and conquered the heathen; the cross which later was cut by the abbots of Glastonbury on their great seal.

One night, so the story goes, King Arthur while being entertained by the nuns of Wearyall in their hostel was summoned in a dream to go to the chapel upon Pons Perilis, and there he was present at the midnight mass wherein Our Lady herself served the altar and gave her Child to the priest to sacrifice.

At the conclusion of that mystical repast she took from her own neck the crystal cross and gave it to the king that in its power and purity he might conquer the heathen. So he no longer fought under the scarlet dragon of Wessex, but under the clear white cross of Our Lady. This was as near as he ever came to the Vision of the Graal.

Standing there, on the crest of Wearyall, and looking back at the red-roofed town among its trees and coombes, all the story of our English Jerusalem is spread out at one's feet; the slow-moving river that guarded the village of the lake-dwellers; the landing-place of Joseph; the chapel of the vigil of the knights; all the story of Avalon touches the long, narrow, whale-backed spit that runs out into the marshes, for it is the land and its ways that make history far more than the will of kings.

7.

The Holy Thorn

JUST within the Abbey precincts, close to an old grey wall warmed by the sun, stands a gnarled hawthorn, scantily leaved and thin of branch, old and feeble. To this shabby and time-worn tree pilgrims from all over the world do reverence, for it is the scion of St. Joseph's staff. It is not, alas, the Staff itself—a Puritan zealot cut that down as an act of piety during the rule of the Protector—nevertheless, it is an immediate descendant, for from the famous tree a slip was taken and planted in the monks' garden within the Abbey wall. There is a brother tree from the same stock, more prosperous looking, and presumably younger, standing in the churchyard of the lovely Church of St. John, and from this tree come each year the mayflowers that, born out of due season, decorate the high altar for the Christmas festival.

A strange story belongs to these two old trees which are not as other trees. It is quite true that in the spring-time they put forth leaf and flower, along with the other English thorns, but in mid-winter, amid cold winds and cold grey skies, there comes another blossoming, and knots of creamy flowers hang amid sear berries and bare boughs.

Botanists tell us that the old trees are strangers in our midst; they are not of the English trinity of 'oak and ash and thorn', but are exiles beside the still meres of the Westland moors. Nevertheless, they forget not Zion, and when the spring wakens in the Holy Land they put forth bud and blossom, for they are Levantine thorns, and the tale of their coming to Glastonbury goes back beyond history into the mist of legend. None others are known in the West save these two trees of Avalon and their scions.

Tradition is in no doubt as to their origin. Their parent was the staff that supported the aged Joseph of Arimathaea, our first missionary. After Our Lord's death, when Christianity was beginning to spread throughout the Near East and along the Mediterranean basin, the Word came to the ancient saint that he should bring the Christ-message to the Islands of the West. And he followed the track of the tin-ships, ever bearing west by north, till he saw before him a hill like Mount Tabor, the Hill of Vision, and there he landed and made his home and told his story to the savage tribes of the matted woods and marshes, who, nevertheless, were not so savage that they could not understand the story of the Christ-child when they heard it; and to the ancient man who came in the name of the Prince of Peace they gave twelve hides of land, rich and well-watered, that he and his brethren might dwell in their midst and tell them the Good News.

On Wearyall hill, the long, low spur jutting out into the marshes, the first firm ground between Avalon and the sea in those days, St. Joseph set foot on English land, and he drove his staff into the warm red Westland soil as he took possession of our islands for the spiritual kingdom of his Lord, a realm not made with hands, eternal in the heavens.

And the kind Westland earth received the worn old staff lovingly, so that life woke anew in the dried fibres; and lo, it budded and blossomed, leaves came forth green and flowers showed creamy-white among the grey winter grasses of the Somerset meadows. So the weary old saint kept his first Christmas there, with the promise of the staff to gladden his heart amid our grey fields and rolling mists and low winter skies. The Glastonbury Thorn was the first Christmas-tree in our islands.

By the miracle of the Blossoming Staff God set His seal upon the mission of St. Joseph. The sign of the hill like Mount Tabor had been fulfilled to him, and now this final miracle could leave no doubt in the minds of any of the little band; with joy they built the first church in Britain, made of withies cut along the banks of the slow Brue and plastered with mud from the ditches that drained the pasture-land about the foot of the Tor.

And their high hope was justified, for the men of marsh and Mendip, and even the fishers of Severn, were glad of the Good News, and welcomed them as those long watched for and well loved.

Here, too, rose one of the first and noblest churches of stone in these islands, for the Westland men, learning the Truth from the lips of one who had learned it from Our Lord, were well taught, and never turned back to the Old Gods again, but loved and worshipped Christ in their hearts and honoured Him with their hands, so that it is said that a man may travel through the length and breadth of the West Country and never be out of the sight of the lovely towers by day nor the sound of sweet bells by night. Indeed, in the old days it was the kindly custom to place a lantern in the church tower at dusk so that wayfarers in the marshes might be guided on their path, and the lantern windows can be seen to this day in many a tower; there are even some churches in which the gracious old custom is still maintained, and a few strokes of the bell rung in the darkness that wanderers may come safe home.

In some of these churchyards there are ancient thorn trees, scions of the scions of the staff of the old saint. The Somerset men of to-day, who bury their dead amid the tangled roots, do not know the story of the traveller from far lands that sojourns among the yews, for the trees, removed from the 'holyest erthe in Englande,' do not retain their habit of a Christmas blooming; but their broad, smooth leaves, of a darker green than our English hawthorn, mark them out from the trees of the hedgerow, even as the dark eyes and olive skins of the old saint and his comrades must have contrasted with the fair skins and grey eyes of the tribes.

But in other churchyards there are young, slender thorn-trees, tenderly guarded and reverenced, brought back as holy relics by the modern pilgrims who go by train and car to ancient Avalon. And although they may not fulfil the tradition of a Christmas flowering away from the kindly island valley of Avalon,

> Where falls not hail or rain or any snow,
> Nor ever wind blows loudly,

nevertheless they bear witness to a renewed care for the

beautiful symbols of holy things. Glastonbury, the Isle of Saints, is once again our English Jerusalem, and from her deep wells are drawn sweet waters of refreshment for the soul. Once again we are realizing the priceless gift of holy places, and the two old trees hear the chanting of hymns as priests and people move in procession from the one to the other through the streets of the red-roofed town. Once again incense drifts through the gnarled branches and copes and vestments shine glorious against their dark leaves, for the Church is remembering her heritage.

8.

Glastonbury of the Monks

THERE are many Glastonburys, and though her ancient walls have never been cast down, like the walls of Troy, her spirit has hidden levels, depth below depth, like the rocks of a mountain range, and in different places these come to the surface. The ancient courts and low-browed doors of her old houses are of the Middle Ages, and the spirit of the medieval Church broods over the centre of the town. The hand of the abbot ruled all the country around, for the Abbey lands stretched far, and grange and steading acknowledged his rule and paid tribute to his barn. The arms of the Abbey can still be seen over the door of many a grey farm-house out on the moors. The rude charity and still ruder justice of the day were administered by him, as the stones of Glastonbury bear witness. Two rows of low-roofed, stone-floored, heavily timbered cottages stand in the town, one for old men, and one for old women, and each has its tiny chapel, for the monks cared for the souls of their pensioners as well as the bodies. The old women live out their lives under the shadow of the Abbey; their gay gardens stretch to its boundaries and the Holy Thorn leans over their wall. At the end of the little gardens is the Chapel of St. Patrick, with its altar of rough masonry. When the angry hands of the Reformation cast down the noble church, the little lowly chapel that ministered to the souls of the old women was left in peace. The great towers that shadowed it fell, but the bell of St. Patrick still calls to prayer to this day.

The great nave of the Abbey stands roofless to the sky, its broken arches soar and its grey walls stand. Where the walls fail, old beeches take up the burden. Its floor is of perfect green, such green as only English turf can give. The West Country sky has a blue of Italian depth, and with the green below and the blue above and the grey stones soaring to meet it, Glastonbury has a magic for the soul that is not found in the churches standing unbroken.

The great building abbots glorified God in the beauty of their Abbey, adding chapel and porch and arch. The Abbey buildings reached from the beautiful cruciform tithing-barn in the south-east to the arched gateway looking upon the market cross to the north-west. Within the great wall to-day cattle graze and cider-apples ripen. The turf is green and close and smooth, as behoves turf of trodden ground. Faint, shadowy lines of ridge and hollow show where the old footings ran. Out in an open field stands the Abbot's Kitchen, memorial of past glories. At each of its four great hearths an ox could be roasted whole.

The design and masonry of the kitchen are as beautiful as those of the church, and it still stands unharmed by time. Its builders were honest men, and solid stone went to its structure. It was not so with the Abbey, alas! The ambition of some of the abbots prompted them to build beyond their resources, and the broken walls to-day show the dishonest rubble of the great piers; where solid masonry should have carried the weight, clay and brickbats were rammed in between facings of worked stone. Noble as the structure looked to the eye, constant buttressing and shoring were needed, and a heavy tax was laid on the successors. It was denied to them to leave their names writ in stone, and they were ceaselessly occupied in keeping intact, lest it collapsed about their ears, the work for which other men got the credit. Finally, the wonderful inverted arches, such as may be seen at Wells Cathedral, were inserted under the great bell-tower. A marvellous piece of masonry, this great figure of eight in stone, springing unsupported and unbuttressed from floor to roof and taking the strain of the tower and its bells.

To the south of the great church were the cloisters, sheltered from the north by the lofty walls of the chancel, open to the sun and the south, for the monks loved to warm their old bones while they paced backwards and forwards in the cloisters, getting up an appetite for the good capon which should line their fair round bellies, if Shakespeare speaks true. There were no doubt plenty of good capons for a monastery that held so much rich Westland soil, but we do not hear charges of laxity against the monks of Glastonbury. They seemed to have lived in peace with all their neighbours save the Bishop of Bath and Wells, who had his own views about their independence and privileges, and the townsfolk bore them no ill-will.

They were noted scholars, and the sons of many noble houses were sent to them to be educated. To the south of the cloister garth was the scriptorium, where the copying of manuscripts was done with such painstaking care and artistry. To the Abbey on its island among the marshes came rare pigments from all the then known world. The murex of the Mediterranean which gave the Tyrian purple, the reds of the East, and even such queer ingredients as ground-up mummies, which were a favourite colouring matter with our forefathers. The lichen of their own apple trees gave them a good yellow, as it does to this day to the many craft-workers of the district.

It was Peter Lightfoot, a monk of the Abbey, who made the wonderful clock now in Wells Cathedral. Not only does it tell the hour and minutes, but the day of the week and the phases of the moon. At each hour a party of knights come out of its works and fight a tourney with a great clashing and clanging, and the ancestors of Gog and Magog are responsible for the chimes. It was a great toy, this wonderful timepiece, and tells us much about the mentality of the man who made it and the abbot who allowed him to.

Out in the fields beyond the Abbot's Kitchen lies a small round pool of time-worn stonework, lily-pads floating on the surface of its water. Here were put the live fish held in readiness for Friday. Out in the marshes towards Meare is an ancient stone structure, ecclesiastical in character, not unlike a small chapel. This was the abbot's fish-house, where the fish taken in the slow streams of the marshes were smoked and stored. Just beyond it are the fields with the low round mounds that mark the dwellings of an ancient people, who also fished those slow streams.

So layer below layer the memories lie asleep in this good land. The monks lived their lives, rich with a hundred interests. Seed-time and harvest did not fail them, nor the innumerable water-springs. Grange and farm and distant pool sent their tribute to the tithing-barn of the abbot. Still we cut stone where the Abbey stone was hewed. Still the timber-wains with their teams come down the narrow lanes. Hides are tanned among the water-meadows to this day, and the osier-beds still yield withies for basket-work. Only the fish are gone with the draining of the marshes.

Medieval piety and medieval learning are in the very air of Glastonbury. The stones of the Abbey are over-thrown, but its spirit lives on like a haunting presence, and many have seen its ghost. Dreaming alone in the quiet of the great roofless church, the ghostly pillars re-form themselves to the inward eye; the high altar shines with its lights and a chanting draws near down the hollow aisles. Then the dream goes, dispelled by the sunlight, and nothing remains but a drifting cloud of incense. Many have smelt the Glastonbury incense that comes suddenly, in great breaths of sweetness.

The spirit of the Abbey lives on, hidden below the surface of the workaday little town with its market-place, and sometimes it breaks through to the surface, heralded by the drifting clouds of incense, and the soul of the watcher is borne away to another world where men prize heaven and beauty.

9.

The Abbey

ON to the breadth of Magdalene Street looks a great gateway. Beside it is a house-front beautiful with fine stone-mullioned windows, from whose eaves the legend of the 'Red Lion' is gradually fading. This is the gatehouse of the Abbey, and it is said that in the chamber over the gate poor old Abbot Whiting, the martyred Abbot of Glastonbury, slept for his last night upon earth after having been taken to Wells 'to be tried and executed', as the official instructions put it, with unintentional irony.

Under the gate, between modern walls, the path leads to the Abbey precincts, and, the barrier being passed, we tread 'the holyest erthe in Englande'.

Acres of smooth green lawn spread before us, perfect turf without spot or blemish, green as an emerald even in the heats of summer, and from the turf rise broken grey walls. Enormous arches soar into the sky, lean to each other, but fail to meet. The keystone is gone, but still they stand, the mighty piers of the bell-tower.

In the old days, before the Brue was harnessed, the soil of Glastonbury was waterlogged and treacherous, and the building abbots were hard put to it to find sure footings for their walls; some of them, too, did not scruple to fill in with rubble instead of honest stone. So the great

bell-tower was a source of anxiety to the monks, and they
inserted under it beautiful hour-glass arches such as can
be seen to-day in Wells Cathedral.   These have fallen, but
the soaring piers still remain.

The long line of the nave is marked to the south by the
great grey wall with its empty window-spaces where once
the painted glass glowed like jewels; to the north there
is no wall left standing, but its place is taken by a line of
noble beeches at whose feet the footings of the lost
chapels are marked out in stone, for the actual footings
themselves are many feet underground.   These are the
lost chapels that were re-discovered through that curious
automatic script which came into the hands of Mr. Bligh
Bond, at one time in charge of the Abbey excavations.

At the far end of this, the longest church in England,
are the footings of the Edgar Chapel, whose existence was
first revealed by the communications of this script, and
whose discovery under a high clay bank was the first
confirmation of an exceedingly interesting psychic experi-
ment.   At its western end is the beautiful Chapel of St.
Joseph, which, so the legend runs, was originally built
round the little wattle church erected by the venerable
hands of the old saint and his companions. But great
fires have devastated Glastonbury Abbey, and many holy
relics perished in them, and the little wattle church, most
precious of relics, is no more.

Until one of the abbots had the dubious inspiration of
constructing a crypt to this chapel, its floor was ornamented
with a marvellous mosaic pavement representing the twelve
signs of the zodiac with the sun in glory in the centre, said
to be in reference to the twelve companions of St. Joseph

of Arimathaea, who built their solitary cells thuswise about the circular church.

The north door of the chapel is ornamented with the quaintest of carvings which tell the story of the Massacre of the Innocents. In one panel we see the Three Wise Kings tucked up in beds much too short for them, with an angel administering a dream. In another, Herod's soldiers, complete in the chain-armour of Norman knights, have got limp infants spitted on their spears like trusses of hay on a pitchfork. All very lurid and convincing to the people of the time, but quaint as a child's story-book to sophisticated moderns.

To the south of the great church is the sunny cloister garth and the under-croft of the scriptorium where the copying of manuscripts was done.

This is all that remains of the departed glories of Glastonbury Abbey, whose abbots were often of royal blood, who gave statesmen and scholars unnumbered to the service of the realm, whose great library was the marvel of the time, whose relics outshone even those of Canterbury and Westminster, and whose soil was so hallowed by the bones of holy men it held in keeping that the old historian called it 'the holyest erthe in Englande'.

Where is this glory departed? Year by year a wise choice of abbots built up this most ancient foundation. There is no record of demoralization or corruption at Glastonbury. Kings enriched it with gifts and nobles sent it their sons to educate. Pilgrims from all England visited it to pray at its shrines and adore the relics they contained. Why are the arches broken, the great roof fallen, and all the glory departed?

The story is too well known to need to be told. There came a day when men sent from London visited Glastonbury Abbey and made a list of all its treasures. The saintly old abbot was dragged on a hurdle to the top of the Tor and there hanged, and the treasures were sent to the king. The monks were dispersed, the lead was stripped from the roof, the carved rood-screen was burnt to melt the bells, and half Somerset used the walls as a quarry. It is said that the road to Wells was paved with Abbey stone, and in many a cottage we can see to this day the stone-mullioned windows, with their graceful pointed Gothic arches, which came out of the Abbey. When old cottages are pulled down it is constantly found that the stones of which they are composed are richly carved, their carved faces being turned inwards and concealed with rubble and plaster and their smooth backs exposed to view.

And why was all this destruction wrought on a beautiful and venerable thing? Why were men dedicated to God's service, who lived in peace with their neighbours, disbanded and driven out to starvation and misery? Because a pagan king with Christian principles wished to reconcile his conscience with his desires.

The Abbey did not languish and die from internal corruption; it fell as a great ship founders, at one moment going on its way, at the next plunging to destruction with all hands.

Therefore it is that in the Abbey we have so clear a sense of our spiritual past, uncorrupted by decay. The spirit of the Abbey lives on, as it is said that the spirit of a man lives on who has died by violence before his time. When death comes gradually through disease the soul prepares for its departure long before it leaves; it loosens its hold little by little, and is often gone before the death-agony begins. Nothing but a chemical life remains in the body, and when that ceases the flesh goes quietly back to earth. Not so when a man is struck down by violence in the full noon of his powers: his soul will not go to its place and rest, for his time had not come.

And Glastonbury Abbey is like a man struck down in his prime. Its ghost walks. All about us in that green nave we feel the movement of life. The spirit of the Abbey is there, alive and energizing. We have only to close our eyes to feel the atmosphere of a great church all about us.

There is spiritual power in Glastonbury. To stand in the centre of the great nave, looking towards the high altar, is like standing waist-deep in a swift mountain stream. Invisible force is rushing past with a streaming movement. Only in one other place and on one other occasion have I felt the like force—at Christmas communion in Westminster Abbey, when, coming out of the transept into the slow-moving file of the waiting communicants it was as if one stepped from the bank of a river into swift-moving water when the central aisle was reached.

What is this pouring power of holy places? Do we not miss much when we abandon the ancient custom of pilgrimage? The Reformation no doubt swept away many abuses in an age that had fallen on corruption, but with the abuses were destroyed also many good things. Some great truths of the spiritual life were forgotten when every man became his own priest.

Whatever may be the explanation thereof, experience proves that there is power in holy places, power to quicken the spiritual life and vitalize the soul with fresh enthusiasm and inspiration. Where strong spiritual emotions have been felt for long periods of time by successive generations of dedicated men or women—especially if they have had among them those who may be reckoned as saints because of their genius for devotion—the mental atmosphere of the place becomes imbued with spiritual forces, and sensitive souls capable of response are deeply stirred thereby when they come into it.

We are all too apt to forget that we have in our own island holy centres of spiritual power which have been sanctified by the lives and deaths of our British saints. Iona, Avalon, Lindisfarne—are not their names 'three sweet symphonies'? And of these three our own Avalon is by common consent the greatest.

First it was sanctified by the coming of Joseph of Arimathaea bringing the Graal, and from that day onwards men and women of sanctified life made it their home. St. Patrick of Ireland dwelt and died there. St. Bride too came thither from Ireland and made her home at Beckary for many years, though finally returning to Ireland to end her life and die. St. David and seven bishops from Wales journeyed to Glastonbury in order to consecrate the first stone church that was built thereat; but in their journey St. David was met by Our Lady herself in a dream, and told that so holy was the soil of Avalon that the church built thereon needed no more consecration, but had already been accepted by her. So St. David came to Glastonbury himself as a pilgrim, and made his

prayer there and returned to Wales. Tradition declares
that the band of pilgrim monks who were massacred by
the tribes at Shapwick while on their way to Glastonbury
were these Welshmen.

Tradition also has a sweet and beautiful story which we
must love for its own sake, even if we cannot believe it to
be history. It is said that the Holy Child Himself came
to Glastonbury as a boy, travelling with the tin-ships, and
that He preached the Gospel to the wild miners of Mendip,
who heard Him with joy. It is this legend that the great
mystic, Blake, refers to in his poem:

> And did those Feet in ancient time
> Walk upon England's mountains green?
> And was the Holy Lamb of God
> In England's pleasant pastures seen?

But although this story may be fable when viewed
from the standpoint of history, it is a spiritual fact when
viewed from the standpoint of the inner life. At Avalon
is the heart of our spiritual life as a race. Here was
guarded the Graal, the last and highest reward of the
knights already trained in all chivalrous perfection at the
Table Round of King Arthur. In the Arthurian Cycle
and Graal legends we have the Mystery Tradition of our
Race.

Arthur and his Queen Guinevere were buried in Glastonbury Abbey, according to tradition, and Edward I
and his Queen Elinor (*Chere Reine*) visited the Abbey
to assist at the translation of their remains from the
monks' graveyard to a tomb beneath the high altar.
Digging was carried out at the spot indicated by tradition,

and when the monks were almost in despair, having dug
to a depth of fourteen feet and found nothing, they came
upon a great oak coffin, buried lid downwards, and when
they had drawn it forth they found upon the hidden side
the inscription: 'Here lies Arthur, King of Britain.' In
the coffin was the skeleton of a very tall and powerful man,
and in the skull thereof were five wounds, all but one
of which had been healed. At the foot of this coffin
was another coffin bearing no name, but which, when
opened, was found to contain the skeleton of a woman
and a great plait of most beautiful golden hair. This
was as it should be, for tradition declared that Queen
Guinevere, after her estrangement from the King, entered
the convent of Amesbury, which is at no great distance
from Glastonbury. Her hair would be cut off when
she became a nun, and it is no strange thing that the
great plait of golden hair her chief beauty, should be
placed in the coffin with her body when it was brought
the few miles over the moors to be laid, not beside, but
at the feet of the husband she had loved and wronged.

St. Dunstan was born at Baltonsborough, a few miles
from Glastonbury, and passed his boyhood in the Abbey;
there too St. Hugh of Lincoln served his novitiate, and
when he wanted masons for the fine stonework of his
great cathedral, he sent for Somerset men.

So they pass before us in procession, the saints of
Avalon, till we come to the pathetic figure of the last
abbot, Richard Whiting, with whose miserable death
upon the Tor the story of the Abbey ends.

Thenceforth all was dispersed and destroyed, and the
ruins fell stone by stone. Grass crept over the pavement,

saplings sprang up in the roofless chapels and grew into trees. Summer and winter, seed-time and harvest went on unchanged, till once again, in the cycle of time, Avalon is revered as a holy place and pilgrims once more visit her shrine with prayer.

10.

The Stones of the Abbey

OLD plans of the Abbey, drawn in quaint perspective, show the wide domain that once was
within its boundaries. The gatehouse, with its
steep roof and chamber over the gate, still looks out on
to the wide sweep of Magdalene Street. From the
row of almshouses with their sunny gardens the monks'
pensioners can still watch the come and go of all the
Abbey business. Part of the great wall that enclosed the
monks' garden is still standing—it towers high above
the narrow alleys behind the main street, snapdragons
and red valerian growing in its crannies. Much of it is
gone, but the footings can still be traced right out to the
Abbey Barn, the wonderful cruciform barn, finely built
of grey, lichen-blotched stone, with the statues of the
four evangelists high up in their niches looking down on
the wagons and cattle.

To everything that the monks built they lent an
ecclesiastical touch; there is no mistaking their handiwork.
Even the domestic offices were built with the same careful
beauty as the great church itself. The Abbot's Kitchen,
still standing, bears witness to their love of beauty and
honest craftsmanship.

It is an octagonal building with a steep pyramidal roof.
Within there are four enormous hearths, each designed to
roast an ox whole. Beside them are smaller ovens built

into the thickness of the wall, presumably for pastries. Nothing could be better designed than the lofty roof of the kitchen for carrying off the heat and fumes of these four furnaces, for no other word can describe them, so vast are they. Whole tree-trunks must have gone to their stoking.

It takes little imagination to people the old grey kitchen with the monastic cook and his scullions, for the great flagstones of the floor bear the marks of their feet. There is something strangely impressive in footworn stone. Nothing so humanizes an ancient building as the shallow troughs in its flagstones worn by human feet.

Among the broken pillars of the undercroft can still be seen the stone channels which served the Abbey for drainage. They were built on the same system that the Romans used in their villas, and they still perform their task, keeping the ground dry and wholesome.

There are wells, too, that served that large concourse of monks with water. Strangely situated they seem to us, being right inside the church itself. One well, reputed to be fed from the famous Blood-spring at the foot of the Tor, is right under St. Joseph's Chapel. The low arch that roofs it, deep down in the darkness at the foot of a narrow, winding stair, is beautifully carved with stone hatchet-work, cut in imitation of the chip-carved wood, marvellously wrought with an axe, which was the prototype of architectural decoration in these isles; the technique of one material being imitated in another before it was realized that scrollwork could be wrought in stone as easily as the angular lines of the hatchet-carving.

To us, who are accustomed to purely utilitarian

domestic offices, it gives much food for thought that the monks should have spent such a wealth of craftsmanship in the unseen parts of their buildings. It proves that they worked to the glory of God rather than to be praised of men, for who save the drawers of water would see the fine carving of the well-head down among the Abbey cellaring?

Outside the boundary-wall of the Abbey are two other buildings intimately connected with the monastic life. Looking up the broad Magdalene Street, on to which the Abbey gate opens, stands the wonderful old Pilgrim Inn, one of the finest examples of Tudor domestic architecture in the country, now known as 'The George', but originally the Abbey hostel where hospitality was dispensed to travellers according to the custom of the monastic houses. Many pilgrims were drawn to Glastonbury by the fame of its relics, and no doubt the Abbot found them a distraction from holy duties, so the hostel was built without the walls, where neither the worldliness nor the fevers of the visitors would infect the monks.

The problem of infection was a serious one during the great epidemics of the Middle Ages; and it was during the Black Death that the Tribunal was built, the beautiful old grey stone building in High Street, half-way between the Pilgrim Inn and St. John's Church. Prisoners were apt to revenge themselves on their judges by communicating to them the infectious diseases that were the fruit of foul prisons; the monks were shrewd enough to realize that to bring a prisoner into the Abbey, however much they might desire his apprehension, might not be an unmixed blessing, so prisoners and pilgrims were kept at a safe distance and the Abbey maintained a clean bill of health.

It is said that there are dungeons below the Tribunal, but they have never been explored; it is not the safest thing in the world to dig among the foundations of ancient houses. Up in the triangular channel underneath the eaves, however, the ancient wattle can still be seen— such wattle as was used in the building of the circular church by St. Joseph and his twelve companions, the first church in these islands, and, so tradition says, the first church to be built above the ground in Europe.

The Tribunal and the Pilgrim Inn have been in un-interrupted use since they were built. The Tribunal has been many things in its day. At one time a sisterhood of nuns made it their home, and their flowing black draperies could be seen passing and re-passing in the narrow streets and entering the low arched doors of the old cottages, carrying the imagination back to the Middle Ages and the Glastonbury of the monks. To-day the Tribunal is a craft-shop where are sold the fascinating products of the artist-craftsmen who abound in this part of the world. The old stone rooms are a perfect background for the hand-spun linens and hand-wrought metals; never did shop and merchandise suit each other more perfectly.

The Pilgrim Inn is also in sympathetic hands; its rooms, with their stone-mullioned windows and erratic floors of huge boards cut from whole trees, its panelling and alleged ghosts, is furnished with fine old furniture that blends with the spirit of the house.

The courtyard where the coaches used to drive in has been roofed over and made into a lounge; but under the rugs that strew its floor the foot can feel irregularities, and if the rugs are turned back, the deep ruts of the coach-wheels can be seen in the flagstones that pave it.

The soaring pillars of the Abbey itself seem remote from human life. They have stood open to the sky so long that the human atmosphere has faded from them; but the ancient stones that bear signs of the daily usage of folk busied with the tasks that we ourselves pursue every day of the week—the sleeping-rooms, the cooking-places of the men who went before us—these things come home to our hearts, and we feel the unbroken line of our national life stretching back into the remote past, and know that it will reach on into the far future and that we ourselves are a part of it.

11.

The Tor

IN the northern part of Somerset, where it borders upon Gloucester, there is a triangular plain, bounded upon two of its sides by the Mendips and the Poldens, and upon the third by the sea. In the centre of this plain rises a strange pyramidal hill crowned with a tower. So strange is this hill, so symmetrical in form and rising so abruptly from the wide-stretching levels, that no one looking upon it for the first time but is impelled to ask what it may be, for it has that subtle thing which, strange as the word may seem when applied to a hill, we cannot call other than personality.

Seen from a distance, the Tor is a perfect pyramid; but as we draw nearer a central hill detaches itself from the crowding foot-hills, and we see that it is shaped like a couchant lion bearing a tower upon its crest, and round the central portion, in three great spirals, sweeps a broad, graded track, known as the Pilgrim Way.

The whole hill seems to radiate a strange and potent influence, whether seen afar off from the top of Mendip or glimpsed unexpectedly from a bedroom window as the curtain is drawn back in the dark. Whether the full moon is sailing serenely in the night sky behind the tower or whether a dark mass blots out the stars, whether the sun is blazing in a sky of Italian blue or shreds of cloud are driving past in storm, the Tor dominates Glastonbury.

The busy little market town at its foot is occupied with the daily life of men, but on the Tor:

> The Old Gods guard their ground,
>   And in her secret heart,
> The heathen kingdom Wilfred found,
>   Dreams, as she dwells apart.

In the centre of this, 'the holyest erthe in Englande', rises the most pagan of hills. For the Tor keeps its spiritual freedom. It has never cried: 'Thou hast conquered, O Galilean.'

Tradition declares that its crest was once crowned by a stone circle like Stonehenge, an open Temple of the Sun, and that the graded way which winds thrice around its cone was the processional way by which the priests of the sun climbed to the high places of their worship.

When the dying paganism handed on the torch to the new faith, the sun-circle was cast down, its great stones broken in pieces and flung into the foundations of the Abbey, so that the new church rose from pagan roots. The well at the foot of the Tor, the dark Blood Well of ancient sacrifice, was made the hiding-place of the sacred Cup; the gracious Christian legend twined about the grim stones of the old faith, the invocation of elemental nature was forgotten, and the beautiful tale of the Graal began.

Round about the sacred Blood Well, so the story runs, certain hermits made their cells. But these holy men were so troubled by the principalities and powers that the ancient ritual had summoned to the Tor that in self-defence they built a church upon its summit and dedicated it to St. Michael, the mighty archangel whose function it is to hold down the powers of the underworld.

But even St. Michael was helpless against the Powers of Darkness, concentrated by ritual, and in the earth-quake of A.D. 1000 the body of the church fell down, leaving only the tower standing. Thus was the Christian symbol of a cruciform church changed into the pagan symbol of an upstanding tower, and the Old Gods held their own.

Over the door that gives entrance to the tower are carved two curious symbols which have endured the stress of storm and fanatical zeal, though the statues of the saints have fallen from their niches.

Upon one side of the lintel is a bas-relief of the soul being weighed in the balance, and upon the other is the semblance of a cow. What are these symbols doing on a Christian tower? Who that has studied the Egyptian *Book of the Dead* does not know the symbol of the soul in the Judgment Hall of Osiris being weighed in the scales against the feather of Truth, with the grim Jackal of the Gods awaiting to devour it if it be found unworthy? And who has not seen there also the cow-goddess Hathor with the moon between her horns? What are these two glyphs doing upon the high tower of Glastonbury Tor?

The Tor is indeed the Hill of Vision for any one whose eyes have the least inclination to open upon another world. Innumerable stories are told about it. There are some who, visiting Glastonbury for the first time, are amazed to see before them a Hill of Dreams which they have already known in sleep. More than one has told of this experience. Many times the tower is reported to have been seen rimmed in light; a warm glow, as of a furnace, beats up from the ground on wild winter nights, and the sound of chanting is heard from the depths of the hill. Towering forms of shadow and light are seen moving among the ancient thorn-trees that clothe the lower slopes, and something which no eye can see drives the grazing cattle down from the heights; and they do not fly from it in panic, but go quietly and orderly at the bidding of the invisible shepherd, who leads them away in order that the Sun-temple on the heights, not made with hands, eternal in the heavens, may be made ready for those who come to worship there. On more than one occasion we who live upon its flank have been called upon to minister comfort and consolation to those who have actually seen what they went to look for.

Wonderful as is the view from the Tor by day when half Somerset lies spread at one's feet, with the far hills of Devon to the south across Bridgwater Bay, and, in clear air after rain, even the hills of Wales to the west, far more wonderful is the sight by night for those who dare to climb in the dark. Most wonderful of all, perhaps, is to climb the Tor at sunset and watch the sun go down over the far Atlantic. From the Tor we see two sunsets— the sun himself in his glory in the west, and the reflection upon the clouds in the eastern sky. To see the moon rising through the rose-pink glow of the low clouds over the darkening marshes is a thing never to be forgotten.

As the lights come out in the town at the foot of the hill, it is seen that they form a five-pointed star, for there are five roads out of Avalon—to Wells, Meare, Street,

Butleigh, and Shepton Mallet—and the houses, following along these roads as men's homes must, clustered most thickly where they leave the town, and becoming fewer as the roads draw off into the marshes, form a perfect star of light about the Tor with its tower.

There is one time above all others when it is well to ascend the Tor at nightfall, and that is at the full moon of the autumnal equinox, round about the Mass of St. Michael. The nights are coming cold then, but the days are still warm with the afterglow of summer, and the cold of the darkness, chilling the warm breath of the meadows, causes a thick but shallow mist to form over the levels. Through this the cattle wade knee-deep as in water, and trees cast shadows in the moonlight, black upon silver. As night closes in the mist deepens. Like the rising tide in an estuary it fills the hollows. Trees and barns slowly drown. Only the few scattered knolls like St. Bride's Beckary remain as islands in the mist. Lights on the far roads flit like fireflies in the white gloom. Gradually they too fade as the mist thickens, and Avalon is an island again.

Local folk call this shallow mist that lies upon the levels the Lake of Wonder. Through it comes slowly the black barge, rowed by the dumb man, bearing the three weeping queens who bring Arthur, wounded unto death at Lyonesse, that he may heal him of his grievous wound in our green coombes among the apple-trees.

Into the Lake of Wonder Sir Bedivere flings the magic sword Excalibur, graven with strange runes in an unknown tongue. And the white arm of the Lady of the

Lake, rising from the rushes, seizes it and draws it under. To this day its jewels, gemming the rusting blade, lie among the marshes, waiting to be found.

All these, and many more, come back to Avalon when the Lake of Wonder rises from its faery springs under the Hunter's Moon.

But I have seen a stranger thing even than the Lake of Wonder by moonlight. There are times when there falls upon the Glastonbury levels what is known locally as the Blight. A strange heaviness that will not turn to thunder is in the summer air. The sun glows dully like a copper disk through the low-lying clouds, and in the oppressive dimness and heat, nerves are on edge with restlessness and uneasiness.

On one such occasion, driven desperate by the oppressiveness of the levels, we set out to climb the Tor. Up and up through densest mist, moving in a circle some ten feet in diameter, shut in by a white wall impenetrable as stone—we climbed to the very summit, and there in a white blindness, came out of the mist as suddenly as a train runs out of a tunnel. The crest of the Tor was above the cloud-line.

The sky was of that deep indigo-blue often seen at Avalon—a blue that should be seen through the boughs of an apple-tree in blossom. From marge to marge no cloud flecked its depths, but below our feet there stretched to the very horizon a rolling, billowing sea of purest white with purple in the hollows. Above our heads was the tower, its shadow flung far out over the cloudy floor. It was as if the world had sunk in the sea and we were the last of mankind. No sound rose through the mist, no bird circled above us. There was nothing but blue sky, grey tower, billowing mist and blazing sun.

There was no air moving. All was still and silent as the moon. Time went by uncounted, till presently a slight air began to stir; soon it strengthened to a breeze. Then the clouds began to move. They rolled and banked into great billows and flowed towards the sea. Faster and faster as the wind freshened they went shouldering past below our feet. Soon long rifts began to open in their mass, and we saw the dark Butleigh woods for a moment, wrapped in deepest shadow. Rifts closed and opened again, and closed again, giving us glimpses of the peat-cuttings over to Ashcott and the red roofs of Street. Then the water-cuts began to show as silver wires through the mist; sounds began to rise up faintly through the thinning cloud—a cock crowing, a dog barking, distant bells. Then the last of the mist rolled back bodily and went in a flying wall towards the coast, and the levels lay spread in golden sunshine. Twice have I seen that from the Tor, and the sight is never to be forgotten.

12.

Glastonbury of Today I

IT is not an easy thing to write of the Glastonbury of to-day, so much human nature goes to the making of it. There is an old saying that little children and fools should never be shown a thing till it is finished. It is a saying that comes from the East, for it is illustrated by the story of the weaver of carpets who sat in his open-fronted shop in the busy market-place. Passers-by watched him at his work and commented on its progress. They pointed to the dingy threads of the spring warp and the innumerable knots, joins, and loose ends. If he had listened to them he would have thrown down his handiwork in disgust and despair. But despite all the hostile criticism and ridicule by which he was surrounded, the old craftsman went on patiently adding knot to knot in the fine, hand-tufted carpet-weaving of the Orient, hundreds of knots to the square inch. Finally, at the end of many moons, the clumsy great loom was creakingly unwound, the ends of the warp were tied, and the glory of the carpet was exposed to the wondering gaze of the crowd. So great was the fame of this carpet, the work of years, that the king sent his vizier to purchase it for the great mosque where its beauty should glorify Allah. The scoffers were too ignorant to realize that a carpet is worked inside out. Only the wise artist-craftsman knew that.

So it is with the world around us. The spirit of the race is pulsating with life. The angels are ascending and descending on Jacob's Ladder, but no one sees them except the artist, and he is unheeded. It is the Mad Hatters in our midst who get a hearing; and they tell us that there is 'Jam yesterday, and jam to-morrow, but never jam to-day'.

History is life seen in perspective. When history is in the making, as it is at Glastonbury, it is impossible to assess it at its real value. One can think of it only as it affects oneself. The wagons bringing stone to the temple claim right of way across one's cabbage-patch; their clumsy wheels creak and shed clods of mire; the wagoners beat the horses and the horses kick the wagoners; a grit gets in one's eye as the master craftsman, working in a fine creative frenzy, sends the chips flying. All these things matter, and matter very much, to the people on the spot.

The world which does homage to the masterpiece does not see the smudged palette and the filthy smock that went to its making.

The history of modern Glastonbury has many stories which in due course will get their telling, but we must wait for the perspective of the receding corridors of history before this can be rightly done. It is not easy for us in the present day to stand back and look at those things which have been achieved as history will look at them, not troubling as to whose feelings have been hurt, whose ideals outraged, or whose rights have been treated cavalierly; but seeing rather the gifts that have been brought to the altar of civilization by the artist-craftsmen of Glastonbury, whether they have wrought in words, sounds, colours, or stone; for history is not concerned with their failures but only with their achievements.

The artist has ever lived with his head among the clouds of his golden visions and his feet deeper sunk in the mire of common clay than his neighbours. The skill of his hands in creating beauty seems ever to be equalled by their fumblings in handling stocks and stones. His neighbours, who are well qualified to assess his ineptitude in the mundane sphere, are not equally able to assess his achievement in the things of the Kingdom, and so no balance is struck.

The artist is penny foolish and pound wise. His clocks never keep time, his accounts never balance. He is God's fool, who sits on the floor of the world and hears:

> The eldest council of things that are—
> The talk of the Three in One.

Glastonbury has ever been the home of men and women who have seen visions. The veil is thin here, and the Unseen comes very near to earth. The very stones of the old town radiate inspiration as a sun-warmed wall feels warm to the touch like a living thing in the dark. Many folk of diverse views have heard the voices of Avalon; for there are two Avalons, the Christian and the pagan—the Avalon of St. Joseph and St. Bride and all the bright story of Christendom, and the other, older Avalon, of Mage Merlin and the Lady of the Lake; and between the two, belonging to both, weaves the shadowy figure of Arthur, Excalibur in his right hand and the Graal in his left.

Some of those who make the Glastonbury pilgrimage come to do reverence to the dust of saints in the serene green nave of the Abbey; some come to open their souls to the fiery forces going up like dark flames from the Tor. Who shall judge between them?

13.

Glastonbury of Today II

THE first stirrings of re-awakening life in Avalon came when the family fortunes of the Jardines threw the Abbey ruins on the market. Many times had the Abbey ruins and the house built from their stone changed hands, seldom passing from father to son. The destructive fingers of the ivy clung to the great stones of the arches, and flowering things grew in the treacherous rubble of the walls, undermining and pulling apart that which they beautified, and Glastonbury Abbey fell stone by stone, unhonoured and untended.

Meanwhile there were those who knew what Glastonbury meant, and they watched and waited, biding their time. The old inn at the foot of the Tor was bought by them as a temporary abiding-place, pending the ripening of their plans. It was a tumbledown hostelry that had fallen on evil days since the mail-coaches no longer came pelting down the perilous hills from Shepton Mallet on their way to the cathedral city of Wells. But with the old inn went something that was highly esteemed by its purchasers. A long, narrow strip of garden ran up the steep coombe to a neglected orchard of gnarled apple-trees, and where garden met orchard there was an ancient well-head. From this well-head a pouring torrent of rust-red water came rushing and leaping down the steep garden. A hundred years ago one of Glastonbury's many seers was told in a dream that the waters of this well had healing properties, and he went there and bathed as bidden, and was cured of his illness. He then put up a bath-house of grey Mendip stone, enclosing two enormous and sinister-looking stone tanks with steps descending into gloom, and announced to the world that a miraculous well had been discovered.

The world, which is ever ready to believe what is pleasing, flocked thither in post-chaises and on foot even from far-away London. And no doubt after the pilgrims had bathed in that icy water in those forbidding tanks they thought no more of their imaginary aches and pains, having now acquired something tangible to worry about. However, after the first enthusiasm wore off, results did not justify expectations, and the water was very cold, so the beginnings of a spa petered out.

Its new owners, however, knew the story of St. Joseph and the Cup of the Last Supper. On the flank of the old inn there arose a tall building of grey dressed stone with a red pantile roof reminiscent of Italy, whence, it is said, its clerical architect drew his inspiration, and, lo, the monks were back at Glastonbury! The cliff-like wall of Chalice Well is a landmark for miles. It has a beauty of its own, with its fine proportions and the old, low, huddled buildings that once were an inn clustered about its foot.

Once again there were watchers beside the Tor, in the very spot where tradition averred that certain anchorites had built their wattle huts and prayed beside the Well. Indeed, the old inn had been called 'The Anchor', a strange name for an inland hostelry; and the antiquarians still argue as to whether its name is a reminiscence of the holy men who once dwelt there, or of the day when the tides reached to Glastonbury and coasting and fishing-boats tied up at the quays of the Brue.

These new anchorites watched patiently beside the Well, training lads for far mission-fields and waiting for the day when the Abbey ruins and the house built from them should once more change hands, as they knew well that they would, for there is always a curse on despoiled Church property, and it never comes down in the direct line of descent.

In due time the day came for which they had waited so patiently, and the Abbey stones were put up to auction. The Church of Rome bid for them, meaning to make of our English Glastonbury another holy centre and place of pilgrimage. But there was a stranger there, a man from the north, whom none knew, and he bid and bid from a bottomless purse, and all other purchasers fell away save the monks. Finally, after all their patient years of waiting, they too gave place to the man with the bottomless purse, and the Abbey was knocked down to the stranger. Then came the revelation as to the identity of the purchaser. The Abbey had been bought for the Church of England! And now, irony of ironies, it is in the care of the Bishop of Bath and Wells. That which the old monks so greatly feared has come upon them, and their inveterate enemy has at last gained control of their ancient liberties.

Had the Church of Rome succeeded in her design, would we have seen another Buckfast Abbey raised by reverent hands to enshrine the grey ruins even as they enshrined the little wattled church? Which is the fairer—carved stone and painted glass, or the smooth green lawns and the trees? Who shall say?

14.

Glastonbury of Today III

THE sale of the Abbey was not the only auction at Glastonbury wherein spiritual values came on the market. Disappointed in their plans, the monks at the Well no longer desired to retain their foothold in Glastonbury, and the monastery also was put up to auction. To that auction came three bidders of importance—one was a manufacturer of woollens, who coveted the holy well for its water-power; another was a wealthy American; and the third was Miss Alice Buckton of *Eagerheart* fame. But although three came to the auction, only two arrived there, for the train bearing the rich American broke down out in the marshes. Avalon would have none of her.

So the bidding lay between the manufacturer of woollen goods and the author of *Eagerheart*. The Holy Well had a certain definite value as a source of water-power, just that, and no more; for if the price of it went above the price of the equivalent horse-power in boilers it became an unprofitable investment.

But as a source of spiritual power it was the pearl of great price, and Miss Buckton sold all that she had and outbid the woollen merchant, while the stranded American sent angry telegrams demanding the postponement of the sale or, alternatively, offering to double the price given by the successful bidder.

But the auctioneer was not amenable, and so the wonderful holy well of St. Joseph and Merlin and the Graal came into the hands of Miss Buckton, who constituted herself its guardian, holding it in trust for all who made the Glastonbury pilgrimage.

A beautiful cover of Somerset oak ornamented with fine wrought ironwork was made to guard the Well from contamination, and Miss Buckton, putting on a cloak of blue Welsh linen with silver clasps, explained its history and symbolism to visitors.

From time to time the wonderful well-chamber is emptied in order that masses of rust-red, filmy fungus may be removed, and it is then possible to climb down a ladder into the mysterious depths and stand where the living sacrifices of the Druids must have stood.

When the fungus is away, the crystal clearness of the water becomes apparent, and fifteen feet below can be seen the bed of blue lias gravel through which it rises, ice-cold from the depths. The massiveness of the masonry also stands revealed. It consists of those cyclopean blocks such as were used by the makers of Stonehenge and Carnac, yet squared and jointed with the accuracy of the builders of the Great Pyramid, and set in the fine hard cement whose secret has been lost with the Romans. Three sides of the top course of masonry consist of a single block, one of those masses of stone that prehistoric man appeared to be able to handle without the aid of machinery.

Who were the builders of the Well? No one knows. They were probably of the same race who handled the mighty masses of Stonehenge and Avebury. It is true

that Christian legends twine about it. But it is far older
than Christ. Its origin goes back to some ancient nature
worship, long since lost to man.

The monastery itself became a guest-house of exceptional interest. Its activities centred about the
person of its warden, Miss Buckton, who endeavoured to
express her ideals through the many activities undertaken
there. Of these the most important artistically was the
annual production of *Eagerheart*, the exquisite little
mystery play which made Miss Buckton famous, and
which is her *magnum opus*. As professional actors
seldom took part in it, the production was naturally
uneven, but the lack of professional 'finish' was more than
compensated by the reverence and earnestness of the
actors, which made of the little West Country town an
English Ober-Ammergau. Miss Buckton had a marvellous gift for taking what lies to hand and bringing out
its latent artistic possibilities, and her stage settings, all
home-made, were of exceptional beauty. Altogether,
Eagerheart, in its Glastonbury production, occupied a
unique place in the modern English theatre.

Many interesting people came to Chalice Well, and
were persuaded to give of their best for the entertain-
ment of all those who gathered there, for the doors
were thrown open to all comers. Good music, classical
dancing, mystery plays, readings, lectures, and many
other activities made Chalice Well a great centre of
interest, not only to its own visitors, but to the towns-
people also, who owed its warden a big debt of gratitude
for the generosity with which she kept open house to all
Somerset.

She had also gathered about her a little group of craft-workers who used the most primitive of traditional methods, dyeing the raw wool with dye-plants collected from the Somerset hedges and lichen scraped off the trees of old orchards; and spinning it with the prehistoric spindle instead of the medieval wheel. The artistic value of such products naturally does not equal that of the more sophisticated schools of handcrafts, but of their human value there can be no question. It was a fascinating sight to see the dye-pot boiling over a fire of sticks in the orchard, and skein after skein of gaily coloured wool hanging to dry on the gnarled old trees, while the steady thud of the looms sounded from a nearby barn. Such things enrich the human spirit, even if they never fail to empty the pocket.

Some quaint pottery was made out of clay dug in the orchard; the primitive kick-wheel was used, and gave surprisingly good results in skilled hands. The whole spirit of design and decoration was primitive, and had a significance of its own, not only because of its naive charm, but in its psychology, for here the fundamental urgings of the human spirit towards beauty expressed themselves in their own way, uninfluenced by convention, and the result was of great interest.

But apart from the value of these things as assessed objectively, they have a subjective value which cannot be reckoned in silver and gold. They enrich the human soul and bring new values into human life. Miss Buckton had the vision which sees this, and much must therefore be forgiven to imperfections of execution, because it is better that human beings should stumblingly feel their way to self-expression through the making of beauty, than that experts should do it for them and present them with a perfection of artistic achievement which they can neither understand nor appreciate. Such skilled work enriches the world of inanimate things because new objects of beauty come into being, but the world of human consciousness is enriched when new ideas dawn upon human souls. Beauty must be wrought from within to without, not from without to within. The material world is enriched by perfection of artistic technique, but the spiritual world is enriched by the muddy strugglings that went on at Miss Buckton's kick-wheel and the spilth of her dye-pot.

'A man's reach must exceed his grasp, or what's a heaven for?' A dream of heaven was brought a little nearer to earth at Chalice Well during its hey-day. 'A stone once more swings to its place in that dread temple of Thy worth.' It is by such stones as these, added one to one, that the New Jerusalem is built.

15.

Glastonbury of Today IV

WITH the sale of the Abbey, Glastonbury seemed to wake from its long sleep, and that stirring of spiritual life began which is working like a ferment with ever-increasing vigour as the years go by. Prophecy is a dangerous trade, but we may hazard the guess that history will look back to our English Jerusalem as the cradle of many things that have gone to enrich the spiritual heritage of our race.

As the modern monks were drawn to the little town among green Westland fields by the legend of St. Joseph and the Chalice and Miss Buckton was drawn by the legend of the Graal, so were two others attracted by Excalibur. Rutland Boughton, one of the greatest of our modern composers, and Reginald Buckley, who, but for his premature death might have won for himself a position among modern poets, collaborated in the foundation of a school of music-drama in the little West-Country town, designing to make of it an English Bayreuth, even as Miss Buckton and her *Eagerheart* made of it an English Ober-Ammergau.

Here it was that the greatest of our English operas first saw the light of day—the mystical *Immortal Hour*, wherein the exquisite and profoundly esoteric Keltic legend of the fairy woman and her mortal lover as told by Fiona Macleod, is given expression in sound by Rutland

Boughton. Then followed the cycle of the Arthurian dramas, the libretti written by Reginald Buckley; and finally there came the sombre tragedy of the *Queen of Cornwall*, adapted from Hardy's great poem.

All these were produced in the Assembly Rooms of Glastonbury, produced as a labour of love, with volunteer workers in the property room, local craftsmen making Excalibur, and painted paper imitating stained-glass in the gaunt windows of the little hall.

Here was artistic history in the making. Many singers who have since become well known made their debut on this humble and somewhat rickety stage, and here when twice a year the festivals took place, music-lovers came from all over the world, and for a brief period the streets of the little town were filled with artistic folk, short-haired women, and long-haired men, all very gay as to garments, and the sounds of the glorious choruses rang out from the windows of all manner of odd places that were in use as practice rooms.

I had the unique privilege of seeing a performance of the *Immortal Hour*, which, timed to fit in with the exigencies of the local buses and trains, began at sunset. The first scene started with broad daylight shining in through the uncurtained windows of the Assembly Rooms. But as it progressed the dusk drew on, till only phantom figures could be seen moving on the stage and the hooting laughter of the shadowy horrors in the magic wood rang out in complete darkness, lit only by the stars that shone strangely brilliant through the skylights of the hall. It was a thing never to be forgotten.

But, alas, the drama school that began with the delicate

mysticism of the *Immortal Hour* and rose through the
noble idealism of the Arthurian cycle, ended with the
grim realism of the *Queen of Cornwall*. It is not yet the
time to tell that tragic story. A great thing was lost to
Glastonbury and to English music, and every one is the
poorer. To exchange recriminations is simple, to deal
justice less easy. Heaven be thanked, it is not our task.
Only can we mourn for immortal beauty lost and a
stillborn dream.

The work of Rutland Boughton led on to that of
Laurence Housman, who has made his home in the
near-by village of Street, and who produced in the
Glastonbury Assembly Rooms his exquisite *Little Plays
of St. Francis*. Intimate and fresh with the Franciscan
simplicity, the primitive setting of the Glastonbury stage
suited them to perfection, and the Ober-Ammergau
spirit of our little Westland town again made itself felt,
with Brother Juniper trundling Mendip stone in a
barrow borrowed from the local builder, and everybody
anxious for the struts of the rickety stage, which re-echoed
thunderously to his progress.

Surely few such country towns have had the privilege
of being the birthplace of so much which is of permanent
value in the artistic history of our race?

To write of the many artist-craftsmen of the district
would take too long; we cannot pass by, however, without mentioning some of them, not only because their
work is of value in the development of English handcrafts, but because of the joy for the lover of beautiful
things and gracious ideals in seeing the things he loves,
like the newly created beasts of whom Milton tells,

rising from the earth of their origin, and pawing to be free. The web half-spun on the loom, the pot warm from the kiln—these things have a bloom which is lost when they become merchandise in a shop.

Out on the high ridge of the Poldens, where the road to Bridgwater climbs to avoid the treacherous marshes of the levels, there is a certain spot that rings hollow to the tread, for underneath are the cellars where a notable highwayman hid his spoils. Near at hand is the old cottage where he made his home. Outside that cottage to-day hangs a bunch of raw fleece on a little gibbet of its own, and this is the trade-sign of a hand-weaver whose loom can be heard thudding within the cottage. Here are produced those grand handspuns that are the joy of the West-Country hunting people.

At Watchett, on the sea-coast, is made a charming grey pottery, quaint squat teapots with spouts of such substance that nothing but a hammer could possibly chip them, a great virtue in these heavy-handed days; plates that could be used without injury to themselves as arguments in the most virulent family disputes, and quaiches and bowls decorated with soft-toned earths like the pottery of the lake-dwellers that is found amid the marshes. Such pottery is not for the fastidious mahogany table with cut-glass and fine napery, but with old oak and gay hand-woven linens it is the most fascinating thing imaginable.

There are many folk who delight to spend their summer holidays in wandering from craft-worker to craft-worker about rural England and picking up examples of their art. Shops they scorn, and will have nothing save what comes out of the workroom straight to their hands, alive with the craftsman's spirit. It is a delightful hobby, this collecting of craftwork straight from the hand of the craftsman, backing one's judgment to pick out things which future generations will esteem. Napoleon, when twitted with his lack of a family tree, declared that he himself would be an ancestor; so can those who pursue this kindly hobby declare that their discoveries, given time, will become antiques. How much better to encourage the craftsman in his lifetime than the auctioneer of two hundred years hence!

And what delightful people they are, these folk who make their dreams come true by the work of their hands. There is a spiritual quality in the hand-made thing that is lacking to the machine-made, however good may be the design, for the man who makes with his hands the thing which he has himself planned, weaving into it his dreams and the many sacrifices for the sake of his art, giving to it of his best, cannot help loving it by the time he has finished it; and the well-loved thing, warmed and worn by human hands, becomes ensouled with a life of its own. It has a distinct personality, and sensitive and sympathetic people are aware of it. The ancients made amulets with ceremonies, and carefully destroyed the instruments of crime because they knew of this curious property of inanimate objects that have made close contact with the human soul. Like many another secret known to the ancients, we have forgotten this in the hurry of modern life, for we seldom handle the hand-made thing. Nevertheless, it is in this that the fascination of craftwork lies; for the things which the artist-craftsman makes are alive and friendly and companionable, and we love them, we know not why. Perhaps something of the artist's soul has gone to the making of them; they are not inanimate matter, but so many elves and gnomes and fairies that, like the toys in Hans Andersen's story, talk among themselves when no human is there to listen.

There is some fine illuminating done at Wells, also hand-printing from woodcuts; and at Clevedon there is some beautiful weaving of silk and wool and linen dyed with vegetable dyes.

Glastonbury, amid its old oaks, has makers of hand-made furniture, including those curious chairs that look so hard and are so comfortable, made after the pattern of one that came from the Abbey: massive chairs, without a nail in them, that take to pieces and pack flat and are put together again with pegs and wedges.

Glastonbury is indeed rich in the things of the human spirit, its dreams and its ideals. It has inspired the makers of many beautiful things, and will inspire many more, for its message to mankind is not yet finished in the giving. More will yet be brought to birth in the beloved Isle of Avalon among our Westland fields.

16.

The Gate of Remembrance

OF all the strange happenings associated with Glastonbury, perhaps the strangest are those told in two books which marked an epoch in psychic research—*The Gate of Remembrance* and *The Hill of Vision*. Mr. Bligh Bond, well known as an architect and restorer of old churches, had been appointed curator of the Abbey ruins upon their purchase by the Church of England at the famous auction. He was interested in psychic research, and was one day sitting with a psychic friend for automatic writing when the communicating entity began to give an account of the ancient glories of Glastonbury Abbey, claiming to be the spirit of one of the monks connected with that foundation, and in Saxon English and dog-Latin and a very crabbed 'hand of write', expressed his views.

Among other things, he told of side-chapels, and especially a chapel behind the sanctuary, no record of which had been preserved in any known document. He gave exact measurements, such as an architect would require, and so intrigued were the two experimenters that, having by virtue of his office access to the Abbey grounds, Mr. Bligh Bond set to work to dig for the lost footings of the unknown chapels described by the dead monk communicating through the hand of his friend.

And, sure enough, he found them, and they were

exactly as described. And not only did they find one chapel, but chapel after chapel, as night after night the old monk answered their questionings in his barbarous jargon.

It is these curious experiments and their results that are recorded in that most fascinating book *The Gate of Remembrance*; and in the *Hill of Vision* are given some very interesting prophecies relating to the War, which were ultimately unhappily justified.

The publication of these books attracted much attention to the little West-Country town, which was already becoming known in connexion with its musical festival and the work of 'Eagerheart' at her hostel of the Holy Well. One cannot help being reminded of the super-circus which had three rings all going at once, and the poor little boy who became permanently cross-eyed in his endeavours not to miss anything. Some of the *Bab Ballads* are also apposite, but in the interests of peace I will refrain from indicating which ones.

Communications from different entities continued to come through, and were justified by the excavations. And not only did they come by the original medium, but from others, including a man well known in literary circles in America, and these too were justified by the subsequent excavations. I have had the privilege of reading a portion of the automatic script in the evening, walking down to the Abbey with Mr. Bond next morning, watching the pegs put into the unbroken turf among the roots of ancient trees, and seen the picks of the excavators strike the forgotten footings in less than twenty minutes. Exactly where the pegs indicated, the footings ran. Not an inch of ground was disturbed needlessly, the clean-cut trench marked out the ancient chapel.

Sceptics said that Mr. Bond had access to unknown manuscripts, but no one ever produced them, and his work on the Abbey foundations is one of the most evidential things in modern psychic research.

Some interesting work was also done with the divining-rod, searching for precious metals; for it was written in the ancient records that when threatened with attack by the Danes, the monks had buried their treasures and then forgotten where they had put them. Two independent diviners, knowing nothing of each other's work, found the same metals at the same places and approximately the same depth.

I had the interesting experience of watching one of these diviners at work. She was a cultured gentle-woman, and water-divining with her was a hobby. Instead of a hazel-rod, she used a very modern contrivance, an aluminium Y-shaped hollow tubular rod, set in bicycle-handles so that it could revolve freely, and equipped with a cyclometer that counted the revolutions it made. There could thus be no question of manipulation, for the rod swung loosely in the handles, which alone were gripped. The reason for this device was that the hands of the diviner used to become badly blistered by the rapid revolutions of the rough hazel-rods she had originally used when she first discovered her gift. When seeking precious metals she would take a piece of the metal she sought in her hand, silver or gold, as the case might be, and when she passed over the spot where its fellows lay hidden, the rod stirred responsively. She judged the depth at which the hidden treasure was concealed by the number of revolutions the rod made, hence the reason for the cyclometer.

The writer attempted to use the rod, but without result until the diviner, coming behind her, took hold of her elbows, and then there ran down her arms a current of electricity so strong as to be decidedly unpleasant, and the rod began to twitch uneasily, though without actually turning over.

All such goings-on, however interesting they might be to those who had no responsibilities in the matter, not unnaturally fluttered the clerical dovecotes, and the trustees of the Abbey began to look with a sour eye on Mr. Bligh Bond and his doings, and after much heart-burning on both sides, his connexion with the Abbey came to an end. It is still a moot question whether the trustees should be regarded as much-abused persons who had warmed a viper in their bosoms, or hens who had hatched out a swan.

Another interesting matter, though not directly connected with the Abbey, may perhaps be mentioned before we pass on to other ground. Mr. Bond's daughter, who had never received any training in draughtsmanship, suddenly began to produce automatic drawings. These were not the usual nebulous efforts of so-called automatists, but remarkable studies of the nude, reminiscent in their detailed precision of the sketch-books of Leonardo da Vinci. They were produced with extraordinary rapidity, without any model or instruction, and without the re-drawing of a single line. How did a young girl come by her knowledge of the lay-on of the muscles of the human form, most intricate of studies? Here was another problem for the sceptics.

But although the figures she drew were anatomically accurate, they were far from human. Strange ethereal forms of nature-spirits and demons with uncanny eyes like star sapphires flew and writhed across her pages.

The walls in the cottage occupied by Miss Bond and her father on the Shepton Mallet road were covered with these strange figures, a most marvellous picture-gallery, until the scandalized incoming tenant exorcized them with a coat of whitewash.

Strange psychic experiences, too, visited her there under the shadow of the Tor, and she has told of them in a very remarkable book, *Avernus*, a book remarkable both for its psychic record and for its literary quality.

Some strange things have happened to more than one person under the shadow of the Tor.

17.

The Finding of the Chalice

A FEW years ago, before the War, there was a certain 'silly season' which was enlivened by long columns and much correspondence in the newspapers concerning the finding of an alleged Chalice at Glastonbury under mysterious circumstances, wherein a pure virgin, led of a dream, discovered an antique cup, believed to be the Graal, in a holy well. This exciting incident was running its course as a nine days' wonder when a letter was received from a reputable gentleman saying that the cup was his property and he himself had placed it where it was found. So the whole affair fell flat and the newspapers concerned in booming it hastily changed the subject.

The actual facts of the matter, so far as they can be ascertained, for folk are secretive in these affairs, are of great interest and curiosity. The story begins with the visit of a certain professional man to Genoa when on his holiday. His father was a connoisseur of glass, and he was in the habit of picking up odd specimens for him, and dispatching them home from abroad. Visiting an antique dealer on this quest, he was shown a shallow dish of archaic design, and told that it had recently been discovered built into the masonry of the chapel of a nunnery which was being pulled down. He bought the dish for a modest price, and dispatched it to England. In return there came a letter from his father in which was said, 'You little realize what you have sent me.'

The death of the older man occurred, however, before the purchaser of the mysterious dish returned to England, so he never heard what the old connoisseur of glass had to say concerning it.

Soon after his return, however, he began to be troubled by a recurring dream which urged, commanded, and even threatened him that he should take this old piece of glass to Glastonbury and place it in a certain well which would be shown to him. Finally, so much did this dream work upon his mind that he did with his treasured dish as he was bidden. He took train to Glastonbury, placed it below the water-level in an old sluice in the fields near the station where under aged thorn-trees the cattle come down to drink, and returned to his home with a lighter heart, telling no man.

But the matter did not end here. Presently another man began to get a recurring dream—a man dedicated to the pursuit of mystic knowledge—and he was told that he was to take with him a pure virgin and go to Avalon, and that in a place which should be revealed to him she should find the Holy Graal. Obeying this counsel, he persuaded his cousin to accompany him, and as instructed in the dream, they went straight to St. Bride's well, the little spring guarded with old stonework near her hermitage of Beckary, the low mound out in the marshes. There they searched the pool, but found nothing.

Disappointed and discouraged, they returned to spend the night at the hostel, intending to return to town next day. But in the night a dream came to the young girl who had acted as seeker in this strange expedition, and she arose in the darkness before dawn, and went again to the well alone, and taking off her clothes under shelter of the thorn-trees, she got bodily into the pool and groped in its trampled mire, seeking that which had been promised. At almost her first step her foot touched something, and out of the mud she drew forth a strange-looking dish, of a coarse bluish glass, with little crosses bedded in its substance.

This curious dish was subsequently shown to authorities on old glass, and they declared it to be one of two things—either a glass made in Syria at the beginning of the Christian era, or else a specimen of the reproductions of this Syrian glass made at Venice in the fourteenth century. In any case, it was a rare and precious thing.

As ill luck would have it, the newspapers got hold of this incident, turned it before behind, and blazoned it abroad; a little premature credulity and much exaggeration being followed by equally premature scepticism and repudiation.

When the two pieces of this curious story are put together, however, and turned right-side up, which was a thing the newspapers never achieved, what is to be made of it? The facts are vouched for by people whose bona fides are beyond question.

At the present time the mysterious Dish is reverently cherished in a little shrine made in its honour by those into whose possession it came.

18.

Avalon and Atlantis

WHEN the Romans came to Britain they found
savage tribes dwelling in stockaded villages in
the dense forests. Roads there were none, save
the perilous tracks that led through the swamps from
village to village. Nevertheless, the Romans were not
the first road-makers in Britain. Over the uplands went
the ways of an ancient civilization which had fallen
to dust and been forgotten ages before the Romans
conquered the Tin Islands.

What the Roman remains are to us, so were these
ancient tracks to them. Wherever the short close turf
of the chalk defied the trees there were the traces of an
ancient, organized civilization upon a vast scale. Its roads,
its guard-houses, its dew-ponds, and, most wonderful of
all, its giant Standing-Stones, which to this day among
the country people are called Sarsen-Stones. The etymo-
logists tell us that the word Sarsen is a corruption of
Saracen, or stranger. Who were the strangers who
erected the great stones?

History cannot tell us, for its records do not reach
beyond the dawn of our civilization. But before that
dawn there was the twilight of another civilization.
History may ignore it; folk-lore may move in circles;
nevertheless the vestiges remain. Great stones on the
uplands and green ways winding across the chalk bear

witness to the works of an ancient people long since fallen on sleep.

There are traditions more ancient than folk-lore, which tell of a Golden Age when the gods walked with men and taught them the arts of civilization. But even these gods themselves were not the first of created things; they had predecessors—giants whom they overcame and whose kingdoms they took by storm. These most ancient and terrible ones, gods of the rocks, were the first of created beings.

Everywhere do we find this tale of an ancient race, this myth of the gods who made the gods in the dim twilight of the dawn of ages.

But there is another story that companions it—the story of a drowned land and lost civilization. The ancient tradition of Chaldea has it, and the songs of our own Keltic tradition are full of it. For us it is the lost land of Lyonesse, whose church bells can be heard ringing out in the Atlantic beyond the stormy coast of Cornwall, where the dark figure of Merlin moves through the mists of legend—a figure that baffled even the makers of the songs that told of his power and wisdom. They knew not whence he came nor what he was.

Merlin was the guardian and teacher of two children, Arthur Pendragon, King of Britain, and Morgan le Fay, the dark Lilith of our island legend, sometimes identified with the Lady of the Lake, and reputed to be the half-sister of Arthur. Who was Merlin with his profound science, and these two children whom he taught—the fairy woman, not of mortal birth, and Arthur, whom the magician bred according to some secret science of his own, regardless of human law?

Here are many threads that have never been unravelled and pieced together. Does there exist a clue that shall reveal the significance of these ancient tales and justify their wisdom, or shall we dismiss them as idle fancies woven to pass away the long hours of darkness around the fires of the tribes of Britain? We may dismiss the tales, but we cannot dismiss the great stones on the uplands nor the ancient roads between them.

Here, then, is another story, one more to add to the fairy fantasy woven about these ancient days of the twilight of our race.

The Egyptian priests, themselves the heirs of a tradition of extreme antiquity, told Plato of an even older civilization, of which their own was the descendant. They told him of a lost land to westward, drowned by the waters of the Atlantic. The ancients accepted these statements for fact unquestioningly; it remained for later ages to cast doubt upon them, and finally to reject them as such stuff as myths are made of.

But have they been finally rejected? There is a steadily increasing body of opinion which is inclined to view the mythical lost continent of the Atlantic as offering the solution of many of the problems of pre-history. The data on which the evidence is based and the conclusions drawn therefrom may be found in many books, I cannot enter upon them here, for they are not germane to my subject. Nevertheless, they indicate that I am not altogether without justification for the pattern in which I have pieced together the fragments of legend that lie buried in 'the holyest erthe in Englande'.

What is my theory, then, to add one more to the

innumerable company of speculations already extant? Let us begin at the very beginning, as the children say when a story is to be told, and tell something of the tale of Lost Atlantis, and see whether it has any bearing on our own island tradition of Merlin and Arthur and the drowned land of Lyonesse.

From the centre of the Atlantic, reaching out towards what is now Central America, so the secret tradition goes, there was a great continent whereon dwelt the Root Race that succeeded the Lemurians and preceded our own. There was a great civilization, built up with the help of the gods who then dwelt among men. There was built the wonderful City of the Golden Gates, concerning which the folk-lore of all races has a tradition. This city, so we are told, was built upon the flanks of an extinct volcano on the sea-coast of this ancient land. Behind it was a plain stretching back to the inland mountain ranges. It was an isolated pyramidal hill, shaped like a truncated cone, with one side, the inland side, sheered off into a precipice. At its base there was a vast concourse of wattle huts in which dwelt the bearers of burdens. On the shoulder of the mountain dwelt the merchant and craftsman castes, and upon its flat top were the palaces and colleges of the sacred clan, which was divided into two branches, the military caste, and the priesthood.

This sacred clan was most carefully segregated from the rest of the population, and its breeding was carried out under the supervision of the priests. As soon as the boys of this clan were of an age to show their dispositions, those who were deemed fit were taken into the sacred colleges to be prepared for the priesthood, and those who

were not suitable for this discipline were sent to the
military colleges to be trained for the army. The maidens
of the sacred stock were guarded with the greatest care,
and were given in marriage to priests or soldiers, according
to their lineage and temperament. So was the heritage of
the sacred clan kept pure, and a carefully selected stock
bred for the development of those rarer powers of the
mind so highly esteemed among the ancients and so little
understood among ourselves—the powers which enabled
the Greeks and Egyptians to discover the basis of modern
astronomy, and the atomic theory of chemistry, and the
cellular structure of organic matter, without the aid of
any of the instruments whose invention modern science
has had to await for its development.

The Atlanteans, the old tradition tells us, were great
navigators, ranging in trade from the Black Sea to the
Pacific; they were also great colonizers, and wherever
they planted their colonies they brought their priests and
their altars. They were Sun-worshippers, and adored the
Lord and Giver of Life in open circular temples, paved
with great flagstones of marble and basalt. They themselves were of giant stature, and they possessed the knowledge of utilizing the latent force in germinating seeds as a
motive power. Their architecture was of the cyclopean
type—great blocks of dressed stone that no primitive man
could have handled.

Now what of our own Avalon in connexion with this
story? Is there any possibility that in the legends of
Merlin and the drowned lands of Lyonesse we are
touching the history of Lost Atlantis? The Atlanteans, so
Plato tells us, were great seafarers and colonizers. Is

there any possibility that Avalon, with its undercurrent of
pagan legend, was originally an Atlantean colony? Is it
possible that Merlin was an Atlantean—a priest-initiate;
and in presiding at the birth of Arthur he was carrying
out the Atlantean custom of the kings bred for wisdom?
In order to bring the higher consciousness of the evolved
Atlantean race into the Celtic tribes of the colonized island,
did Merlin, in defiance of the strict laws of the sacred
clan, and in pursuit of ends of his own, cross the Atlantean
stock on the Celt, and so breed Arthur? And was Morgan
le Fay, the half-sister of Arthur, the witch-woman learned
in all sciences, with her name derived from the Celtic
word for sea, a pure-bred Atlantean, the British-born
daughter of the sea-people?

Welsh legend is full of stories of drowned lands; and
Lyonesse, beyond the coast of Cornwall, is a tradition of
the Cornish Celts. Is it possible that these drowned lands
are the Lost Atlantis? Did the Celts learn of that ancient
civilization from the adventurous navigators who came to
them for trade and settled among them as colonists? It
is noteworthy in this respect that the peculiar combination
of consonants, Tl, which occurs in the word Atlantis is
very characteristic of the languages of the aborigines of
Central America, and that a similar sound exists in the
initial Ll of the Welsh language, which is pronounced as
a guttural click.

It is also noteworthy that the spread of the Arthurian
legends corresponds with the distribution of the standing-
stones of the ancient Sun-worship.

Do we owe the Green Roads of England, winding over
the chalk, to this ancient race of seafarers who colonized

the southern half of Britain and planted their trading-posts along the west coast of Scotland? Was it they who raised the cyclopean stones, so closely resembling those found standing to-day in the virgin forests of Central America?

Is the streak of psychism that runs through the Celtic race due to the Atlantean blood introduced by the daring experiments of Merlin, the Atlantean initiate who had thrown in his lot with the island peoples after his own race was sunk in the sea?

One more curious point may be referred to here, and its value and significance left to the discernment of the reader. Those who have seen the famous Glastonbury Tor, about which so many legends gather, are always perplexed as to whether it is natural or artificial. Its pyramidal form, set in the centre of a great plain, is almost too good to be true—too appropriate to be the unaided work of Nature. Viewed from near at hand, a terraced track can clearly be seen winding in three tiers round the cone of the Tor, and this is indisputably the work of man. Who were they who worshipped in high places and climbed to them by a processional route?

It is well known that the ancients delighted to build their colonial cities upon the same plan as the mother city in the land of their race. Is it possible that our strange pyramidal hill, with its truncated top and its inland side as steep as earth will stand, may have been wrought to that likeness by human hands in memory of the sacred mountain of the mother continent? Here and there about the plain are rounded hills, still called islands locally—hills with no rocky skeleton, but of boulder clay, left behind by some eddy of the Severn before the silting

sands had narrowed its channel. It would not be a difficult matter to take such a mound of clay, and with no other
tools than picks and baskets, mould it to the desired shape.

Tradition tells that the Tor was indeed a high place of
the ancient Sun-worship, and that a circle of stones like
a miniature Stonehenge once stood upon its crest. These
stones were overthrown when the worship of the Son
supplanted that of the Sun, but so strong were the forces
generated in the spot sacred to the rites of an older race
that a church dedicated to St. Michael had to be erected
upon the spot in order to keep down the dark influences
of the pagan worship. These churches to St. Michael,
built upon the tops of hills, which certainly could not
have been for the convenience of the parishioners, are
characteristic of districts where the ancient Sun-worship
is known to have flourished. Legends of Arthur, standing-
stones, and hill-top churches to St. Michael all seem to go
together.

St. Michael is always represented as treading upon a
serpent; he is the mighty archangel of the south in
magical invocations, and to the south is assigned the
element of fire. Here again we have a curious link. The
Atlanteans were Sun-worshippers, and fire is the mundane
symbol of the sun. Its sacred quarter is the south, just
as the sacred quarter of Christianity is the east. The
serpent is a symbol of two things—of wisdom and of evil.
May it not be that the serpent, in its dual aspect, represents
the ancient wisdom of an older race, a wisdom fallen on
corruption, and therefore evil to a regenerated faith, yet,
nevertheless, a mine of the profoundest knowledge?

Michael, the Christian saint, is a member of an older

hierarchy; he is the mighty regent of the element of fire. Who but he should be implored to hold down the serpent of fire-worship, fallen on decadence?

There are no standing-stones left now upon the Tor; but tradition asserts that they were broken up and used in the foundations of the Abbey; and, indeed, there are stones found in the Abbey which were cut in no local rock and are of a hardness to turn the tools of the local masons. May not these be the fragments of the ancient sarsens, the Stones of the Strangers, who used for their temples the mighty boulders of an extreme hardness which occur in chalk where silicates have mingled with the sand, and which form the 'Grey Wethers' of many an upland pasture?

Whether tradition speaks true or not, there exists at the foot of the Tor the prehistoric well-head wrought of just such cyclopean blocks as were used by the builders of Stonehenge, Carnac, and the buried temples of the Mayas and Toltecs. In the well-chamber is the niche for human sacrifice, the water-sacrifice of a sea-people; and we are told that it was the love of the Atlanteans for human sacrifice and black magic of the basest kind which brought about their downfall and led to the destruction of their land. Where lost Atlantis sank there is the deepest gulf in all the oceans, to this day an unplumbed abyss; and over it floats the Sargasso Sea, a vast island of sea-weed so dense that gulls alight upon its surface and ships lay their course to avoid it.

All this is speculation, not history; modern myth-making, not research. But standing alone upon the Tor, when the Lake of Wonder all but closes over it, one cannot forget the end of Lost Atlantas.

19.

The Vision of Avalon

THE atmosphere of Glastonbury is like a fugue with the threads of many tunes running through it, wherein now one comes to the surface, and now another, but all are there all the time, weaving a background of harmony below harmony to the *motif* of the moment.

It is this intricate counterpoint of the Glastonbury atmosphere that has puzzled many people. For Avalon cannot be claimed by any sect as their private sanctuary. It belongs neither to artist nor to Anglican; neither to psychic nor to pagan. All these have their part in Avalon, and none can deny the rest.

It is not for its historical significance that Glastonbury is of importance to the spiritual life of our race to-day. Many places are rich in history and legend, but they are not 'the holyest erthe in Englande'. Glastonbury is a spiritual volcano wherein the fire that is at the heart of the British race breaks through and flames to heaven.

There are times in the history of races when the things of the inner life come to the surface and find expression, and from these rendings of the veil the light of the sanctuary pours forth. To them we look when we seek inspiration. Glastonbury is rarely rich in these things. Here we find holy relics of many sides of the soul's experience. The deep, remote past of our race is here. Through the valleys of Avalon moves an invisible pageant in an endless procession. The darkness before the dawn is shot through by the magic of Merlin the Atlantean. The dark wild men of the mere go past, fierce eyes gleaming under matted hair. After them come the white-robed Druids with their golden sickles, bearing the holy mistletoe and followed by the captives taken in battle, destined for the sacrificial niche in the Holy Well. Then comes the bowed figure of old St. Joseph, frail and solitary, bearing the Cup. King Arthur rides forth, a strong man in his strength, about his neck the crystal cross which was given him by the Mother of God at Beckary, Excalibur at his side. Guinevere rides beside him in her beauty, her golden hair flowing over her shoulders. The time has not yet come when the shorn plait shall lie in the desolate coffin of the shamed queen who is buried, not at her husband's side, but at his feet. Behind them follows the Lady of the Lake, seen as if through deep water, waiting the time when Arthur shall return to her after the last battle, borne in the black barge, watched by the weeping queens, and Excalibur shall come back into her hands, lost to men for ever.

And after all these follow three maidens robed in white, and amid them a glory that is not of any earthly fire—a glory long gone from men because of their wickedness, caught up to the heavenly city of Arras, some say, but others, buried among the green fields of Glaston-bury.

Then the dreams fade and memory begins. All the

pageant of medieval England goes past us as we look into the mirror of time at Avalon.

> Sometimes a troop of damsels glad,
> An abbot on an ambling pad,
> Sometimes a curly shepherd-lad,
> Or long-haired page in crimson clad,
>   Goes by to towered Camelot;
> And sometimes through the mirror blue
> The knights come riding two and two . . .

Sir Lancelot seeking one thing and Sir Galahad another, still they come to Avalon.

Through the magic mirror the long procession winds— the lowly anchorites, burning with a frenzied zeal, the learned and pious Benedictines whose great building abbots gave beauty to English fields; and, last of all, an old man bound to a hurdle, dragged at the heels of a heavy farm-horse; and after that, fallen towers and roofless walls and darkness.

Excalibur has returned to the heart of the waters. The Graal has gone to its own place, the temple not made with hands, eternal in the heavens. The Abbey walls have fallen. The pageant is over.

The dream passes and the light of common day returns. The cry of cocks on distant farms, the bark of dogs, the bleat of lambs, the smell of peat-smoke and apple-blossom blended—all that makes our Westland spring flows in through the five senses.

But the memory of other things remains. What might there not be for us if we would revive the old-time custom of pilgrimage to holy places at holy seasons? There are tides in the inner life, and on the crest of their flood we are very near to heaven. There are times when the power-tides of the Unseen flow strongly down upon our earth, and there are also places upon her surface where the channels are open and they come through in their fullness of power. This was known to them of old time, who had much wisdom that we have forgotten, and they availed themselves of both times and places when they sought to awaken the higher consciousness.

Every race has its holy centres, places where the Veil is thin; these places were developed by the wisdom of the past until a powerful spiritual atmosphere was engendered there, and consciousness could easily open to the subtler planes where the Messengers of God came to meet it. The standing-stones of a forgotten Sun-worship remain at many a spot in our islands, and any sensitive soul will be able to feel the atmosphere of ancient power that still hangs over them—whether it be the blood-stained aura of Stonehenge or the vibrant, sunlit glow of Avebury.

Do not let it be forgotten that there is a native Mystery Tradition of our race which has its nature aspect in the Sun-worship of the Druids and the beautiful fairy-lore of the Celts, its philosophical aspect in the traditions of alchemy, and its spiritual aspect in the Hidden Church of the Holy Graal, the Church behind the Church, not made with hands, eternal in the heavens. All these have their holy places, mounts, and pools of initiation, which are part of our spiritual inheritance. Let those who follow the Inner Way study our native tradition, and re-discover and re-sanctify its holy places; let them make pilgrimage thereto at the times when the power descends and spiritual forces are rushing in like the tide up an estuary and 'every common bush afire with God'. Let them keep vigil in the high places when the cosmic tides are flowing, and the Powers of the Unseen are changing guard and the rituals of the Invisible Church are being worked near the earth.

20.

The Graal and the Chalice

Before King Arthur's knights set forth on their quest of the Holy Graal, they received the Sacrament. If we consider this point carefully, as we should consider all points in a mystical story, we shall find that it yields much food for thought. Why should those who were able to receive the Chalice at tha altar, seek also the Graal? What more had the Graal to give than the Chalice could bestow? The legend points us to a mystic interpretation of the Eucharist. It shows us that in order to make our communion a spiritual experience, we have to do something more than present ourselves kneeling at the altar rails and receive into our hands a cup blessed by the priest; we have to go forth on a quest of our own, and find for ourselves the actual Cup out of which Our Lord drank the wine of life. Not otherwise can the potentialities of the Chalice become for us the actualities of mystical experience.

The Graal is the prototype of the Chalice, and it is from the Graal that the Chalice draws its validity. If there had been no Last Supper, there could have been no Eucharist. Nevertheless, the Eucharist is more than a commemoration. Our Lord asked of those who desired to share a place in His Kingdom whether they could drink of the Cup He drank of, and be baptised with the baptism He had been baptised with. We know what that baptism was, it was the descent of the Holy Spirit in the likeness of a Dove. The Dove was but a symbol under which finite senses apprehended the manifestation of the flaming power of the Third aspect of the Logos, and the Cup is equally the symbolic equation of the inner experiences Our Lord went through in the cosmic act which redeemed and regenerated mankind. The Crucifixion at the hands of Roman authority was but the material manifestation of the spiritual struggle that was going on. It was not the spilling of the blood of Jesus of Nazareth that redeemed mankind, but the outpouring of spiritual power from the mind of Jesus the Christ.

Behind every material object used in ritual there is a spiritual prototype. The spiritual prototype is created by an experience which has been undergone by a living spiritual being. Just as a tragedy may cause a place to be 'haunted' because the intense emotion there experienced remains in the mental atmosphere, so any great spiritual experience, especially when undertaken vicariously of set purpose, creates a thought-form charged with spiritual potency. Herein lies the power, not only of Our Lord's supreme sacrifice upon the Cross, but also, in their degree, of the penances and martyrdoms of the saints. Thought-forms are created by the dedicated vicarious suffering which is transmuted into spiritual power.

By means of the physical symbol, whether it be Cross or Chalice or relic of the saint, thought is focussed upon the sacrificial act. We contact the thought-form, and its stored-up potency discharged into our souls. We are reminded of the spiritual quality which motivated the sacrifice, and the corresponding quality is stirred in our own hearts. We are stimulated by an inspiring example to 'go and do likewise' in our degree. The Cross is only valid for us insofar as we crucify the lower self and its lusts. The Chalice is only valid for us insofar as Christ is risen in our hearts, and we are striving to realise the Christ-life.

Unless we can share in the inner life of a symbol, its outer form will convey nothing to us. Unless we have made a voluntary sacrifice for pity's sake, we will learn little from meditation on the Cross; unless we have felt the burning light of a living spiritual contact quickening our hearts, we shall receive nothing from the Chalice. The consecrating words of the priest make a cup into a Chalice, but it is only the consecrating consciousness of the communicant which can change the Chalice into the Graal.

Like King Arthur's knights, we must not rest content with the Chalice in the chapel, but go forth in quest of those great adventures of the soul which shall bring us at last to partake of the Graal in the Church, not made with hands, eternal in the Heavens.

Epilogue

AND what of Glastonbury of to-day? Chalice Well is a boys' school. Bligh Bond is in America, secretary of the American Society for Psychic Research; the excavations at the Abbey are no longer directed by the spirits of the old monks but by learned archaeologists, who drive deep trenches here, there and everywhere; one sometimes wonders whether what they find is of as great worth as the smooth green of the perfect turf used to be. Everything is admirably cared for and labelled; and I know that wallflowers, and snapdragons, and red valerian ought not to be allowed to grow on old ruins, because their roots tear the stones apart; but, somehow, one looks back on the old, untidy, thrilling days with regret.

All that is left is Joe, who used to care for the perfect turf, and who tells tales of ancient glories to sympathetic listeners. They say that men who tend horses grow like them; Joe only needs a robe and a cowl and a rope round his middle to be the living prototype of all the jolly old monks of medieval story. He no longer tends the turf now that a motor-mower has arrived, but, most appropriately, presides over the Abott's Kitchen, the noblest lay brother of them all, and a very old friend of mine. I believe that he and I are the last survivors of the great days of Glastonbury.

The school of music-drama, founded by Rutland
Boughton in the big house in Bovetown, after the vicissi-
tudes to which all artistic enterprises are liable, came to an
end, its gaily clad and unconventional students no longer
bring a torch of Montmartre to our sober West-
Country streets, to the great scandal of the local yokels.
Fame has come to its founder; and though we cannot
forget that his students went about without hats, and
even without stockings, we are beginning to be proud of
his association with the town. When he is dead we shall
be very proud of him.

The British Israelites, who also esteem Glastonbury as
a holy place, opened a centre in the house that was once
occupied by Bligh Bond; but that, too, came to an end.
In fact, the Abbey ruins and my guest-house are the only
enterprises in Glastonbury that have stood the test of time.

The last thing of interest to happen here was the end
of the world, which has now occurred three times.
Glastonbury is very conveniently situated for this event,
for it has been prophesied that the top of the Tor will
stick out of the waters when the end comes, and all who
gather thereon shall be saved. People have come to live
in Glastonbury for this reason, and whenever the date for
the end of the world is announced they rush home from
their holidays, and pack picnic baskets, and put them
handy in the hall. Two ladies once gave away all their
winter woollies because the end of the world had been
prophesied for a date early in September, and when
November came, and no end of the world, had to ask for
them back again, to the great disgust of the recipient, who
had now missed the July sales.

Mr. Powis makes use of this prophecy in his book, *Glastonbury Romance*, which has fluttered our local dove-cots to a painful extent. Do we behave like that at Glastonbury? I hadn't noticed it. I must have missed a lot. I am afraid that if people make the Glastonbury pilgrimage, expecting to find Glastonbury romance at the end of it, they will be disappointed. We do not quite come up to Mr. Powis's specifications.

Having had so much to say about every one else, I had almost omitted to mention myself, though I hardly know whether I should be classed as one of the local celebrities or one of the local sights; probably the latter, when I am gardening.

In the hey-day of Glastonbury, when it was the English Bayreuth, we used to say that there dwelt in Glastonbury the Glastonburians and the Avalonians; the Glastonburians were those who only knew the place as a market town and a tourist centre, and the Avalonians were those who were in touch with its spiritual life.

I believe that I am the last of the Avalonians, of those who were drawn to Glastonbury as a centre of ever-renewed spiritual and artistic inspiration, and the story of my doings is quite as quaint as the rest of the Glastonbury romances I have chronicled.

Nowadays, every other house has at least beds for cyclists, but in the good old days accommodation was limited and rather sketchy. And I lifted up my voice in woe and lamentation that this should be so on 'the holyest erthe in England', and someone suddenly presented me with a forty-foot army hut from a camp that was being broken up in the neighbourhood.

Needless to say, a forty-foot hut is not the kind of gift one looks in the mouth, and quite undeterred by the fact that I had nowhere to put it, I accepted it, and the next thing I knew was that it was sitting at the station ticking up tuppences for demurrage; and a forty-foot hut can tick them up pretty fast.

I ran round the town with that hut practically under my arm, looking for a place to put it down, till every one was sorry for me. It is well known that there is a special providence that looks after drunkards, little children, and fools, and it took me in hand, and, lo, there is my hut high up on the side of the Tor, standing firm to this day.

We made of it a hostel for Avalonians, choice spirits who did not mind the climb. We have stuck bits on to it before and behind, and though the accommodation is still sketchy and limited, and we do not recommend it to the sophisticated, it extends a welcome to all who are Avalonians at heart.

Looking out over the roofs from our high veranda, I often wonder whether the life of Avalon will ever stir again, or whether we shall be no more than a tourist show and a market town. Will these dead bones come together, bone to his bone, as they did at Buckfastleigh? There is talk of a great new abbey to rise under the shadow of the old. Every summer at midsummer's day a high cross of larch-poles stands on the Tor behind us, gaunt against the sky; and a long procession winds up, monks and nuns and Children of Mary, and the sound of singing comes to us, and a man's voice preaching fervently.

If any place could become the English Lourdes it is our Avalon. Glastonbury has done her fair share of stoning the prophets, but I fancy the Holy Roman Church is made of sterner stuff than Bligh Bond with his other-world visions and Rutland Boughton with his dream of beauty; and I, for one, hope she will make good her footing, and, impenitent heathen though I am, that I shall hear her Angelus from my high veranda.

Chalice Orchard,
Well-House Lane.

Books About Glastonbury

THERE are two books to which the author must acknowledge indebtedness, and to which the reader should turn if he wants fact and tradition after the shadows and dreams of these pages.

For history they should go to *Glastonbury, the English Jerusalem*, by the Rev. C. L. Marsden; and for legend to *The Glories of Glastonbury*, by Armine le S. Campbell. Both books to slip into the pocket and dip into while wandering about the streets of the town or the paths of the coombes around the Tor.

For those who would capture the spirit of our holy places there is a book delightful beyond all others, *The Priest of the Ideal*, by Stephen Graham. And for the evocation of the visionary pageant of the past we can use *The Ballad of the White Horse*, by G. K. Chesterton, Tennyson's *Idylls of the King*, and Fiona McCleod's *Immortal Hour*.

Finally, in *The Mysteries of Britain*, by Lewis Spence, we touch the very roots of our island tradition.

These seven books should be in the scrip of every pilgrim who takes the road to Avalon, and if he can read in them and have no glimpse of the Invisible Pageant, he is unworthy to set foot on such 'holy erthe'.

Dion Fortune's

PSYCHIC SELF-DEFENCE

A Study in
Occult Pathology and Criminality

PSYCHIC SELF-DEFENCE

Can you recognise the seven sinister signs of psychic attack? Are you aware of the reality behind the ancient legends of the vampire? Do you realise the risks involved in ceremonial magic? These are just three of the subjects exhaustively discussed in one of the most unusual and remarkable publications ever to be offered to the British public. **Dion Fortune,** a practising occultist and natural psychic, analyses hauntings; modern witchcraft; the pathology of non-human contacts; and the elusive psychic element which appears in mental illness; then, even more importantly, details in page after page, the occult means by which you can *safeguard yourself completely from psychic attack.*

THE COSMIC DOCTRINE

Dion Fortune. Timely re-issue of one of the source books of the Society of the Inner Light, in which author records esoteric teachings which she claimed to have received from one of the 'Greater Masters', a discarnate philosopher on the Inner Planes. These revelations are designed to induce a deeper understanding of Cosmic Law. Readers should experience a significant expansion of consciousness and occult knowledge if they reinforce their perusal of the book with frequent periods of study and meditation.

Dion Fortune's
THE ESOTERIC PHILOSOPHY
OF LOVE AND MARRIAGE

and
THE PROBLEM OF PURITY

THE ESOTERIC PHILOSOPHY OF LOVE AND MARRIAGE

Dion Fortune. Esoteric science divides matter into Seven Planes of Manifestation. Man is composed of substances drawn from each plane and thus has seven different aspects to his nature. From this premise Dion Fortune outlines the esoteric doctrines in general, and then provides a more detailed account of their teachings relating to sex. She demonstrates that the higher aspects of sex are essential to the development of the perfect man, and warns of the dangers which may attend ignorant handling of unseen forces. To the esotericist, sex in its sevenfold scope is a source of energy rather than a temptation.

The Life and Magic of Dion Fortune
Alan Richardson

PRIESTESS

The Life and Magic of Dion Fortune

' *In the meantime I had my dream of moon magic and sea-palaces, and day by day I lived in another dimension, where I had that which I knew I should never have on earth, and I was very happy.* '

Born Violet Firth on December 6th 1890, Dion Fortune was to become one of the most luminous and striking personalities of this twentieth century, and womanhood's answer to Aleister Crowley. In this fascinating volume Alan Richardson presents the first full biography of this powerful psychic and medium, obsessed with the study of magic. *She hid behind a veil of secrecy yet still succeeded in becoming a cult figure with a vast following even today, 40 years after her death.*